Praise for *The Habit of Poetry*

"In this wide-ranging and erudite study of a previously neglected subject, Nick Ripatrazone has uncovered troves of valuable cultural artifacts from the American Catholic literary tradition—and also reminded us of the lyrical mastery possessed by these women religious in their written work. *The Habit of Poetry* is a treasure both for the everyday reader and for the scholar of American Catholic history and culture."

—James T. Keane, senior editor, *America Magazine*

"Nick Ripatrazone's *The Habit of Poetry* does us a great service in retrieving an important thread in the fabric of American Catholic literature of the twentieth century, the poetry of women religious whose talent and skill were recognized by both secular and religious critics. Women such as Madeleva Wolff, Jessica Powers, and Mary Bernetta Quinn, to name just a few of the nuns highlighted in this collection, found in their contemplative experience a way to negotiate both their commitments to religious life and their desire for poetic expression about modern life. In their published poems as well as in their correspondence with others, they were part of a larger conversation on the Catholic imagination at work in mid-century American arts and letters. This book had me searching the internet to find their poetry."

—Mark Bosco, SJ, Georgetown University,
author of *Graham Greene's Catholic Imagination*

"Since the Middle Ages, sisters and nuns have used religious life as a source of creative inspiration. In *The Habit of Poetry*, Nick Ripatrazone introduces us to an unlikely cast of characters: a group of mid-twentieth-century women who wrote dazzling, complicated, contemplative poetry and who corresponded with and befriended some of the greatest writers of their day. These women also happened to be sisters and nuns. Balancing engrossing biography and skilled literary criticism, Ripatrazone's book offers us a snapshot of a surprising literary movement largely forgotten until now."

—Kaya Oakes, author of *The Defiant Middle*

The Habit of Poetry

The Habit of Poetry

of Poetry

The Literary Lives of Nuns
in Mid-century America

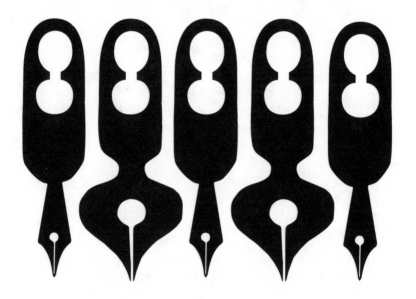

Nick Ripatrazone

Fortress Press
Minneapolis

THE HABIT OF POETRY
The Literary Lives of Nuns in Mid-century America

Copyright © 2023 Nick Ripatrazone. Printed by Fortress Press, an imprint of 1517 Media. All rights reserved. Except for brief quotations in critical articles or reviews, no part of this book may be reproduced in any manner without prior written permission from the publisher. Email copyright@1517.media or write to Permissions, Fortress Press, PO Box 1209, Minneapolis, MN 55440-1209.

Cover design and illustration: Kristin Miller

Print ISBN: 978-1-5064-7112-9
eBook ISBN: 978-1-5064-7113-6

For Jennifer, Amelia, and Olivia

CONTENTS

Preface
Impossible, Edifying Precedents   ix

Acknowledgments   xix

Introduction
Sister Mary Madeleva Wolff: Measured Ambition   1

1 Jessica Powers: Pastoral Mystic   19
2 Sister Mary Bernetta Quinn: Woman of Letters   31
3 Madeline DeFrees: The Springs of Silence   45
4 Sister Maura Eichner: Kenotic Teacher   61

Conclusion
Sister Mary Francis: The Habit of Perfection   77

Notes   91

Bibliography   111

Index   121

PREFACE

Impossible, Edifying Precedents

The iconic seventh-century story about Cædmon, a cowherd who became the first English poet, has inspired generations of storytellers—including Denise Levertov. In her imagining of the tale, Cædmon escapes a night of communal song at the monastery where he worked, and instead seeks refuge "back to the barn / to be with the warm beasts, / dumb among body sounds / of the simple ones." Both "home and lonely," Cædmon was content until an angel appeared, "light effacing / my feeble beam." The angel's fire "touched my lips and scorched my tongue," and then, lit with inspiration, Cædmon soon spoke in poetry.[1]

Levertov wrote of Cædmon during her "gradual and continuous" conversion to Catholicism during the 1980s, a journey sustained by a life in poetry.[2] The work of faith—and faith itself—was never easy. "I have just enough faith to believe it exists," Levertov wrote. "To imagine it."[3] She found the writing of poetry to be spiritually generative. One piece in particular, "Mass for the Day of St. Thomas Didymus," "began as an experiment in structure"—very much "an agnostic Mass."[4] Yet when she reached the Agnus Dei section, she discovered that she had "a different relationship to the material and liturgical form from that in which I had begun."[5] Levertov realized that the "imagination of faith acts as yeast in my life as a writer."[6] Much like Cædmon, Levertov was illuminated, charged by faith to write poetry.

Levertov's arresting poem about her poetic predecessor captures what Gerard Manley Hopkins called "the one rapture of inspiration," the poet's spirit born of religious fire. While this dramatic moment is worthy of poetic appreciation and rendering, there would be no Cædmon the poet was it not for a nun.[7]

In the English monk Bede's telling of the story, Cædmon received his first verses in a dream, and then continued the composition once awake. As a mere cowherd, he would not have direct access to the abbess of the monastery, so he had to tell his superior, the reeve, about "the gift he had received."[8] The nun listened to Cædmon's testimony, and made him repeat his verses for a group of scholars, who further "expounded to him a passage of sacred history or doctrine, enjoining upon him, if he could, to put it into verse."[9] After accomplishing that task, the abbess, "joyfully recognizing the grace of God in the man, instructed him to quit the secular habit, and take upon him monastic vows."[10] The rest, of course, is poetic history—and myth.

In the same way that Cædmon was divinely inspired, we might consider this abbess as imbued with wisdom from God—that she would listen to this cowherd's unlikely tale, with a radical claim as its foundation. Yet Bede does not name her. To be clear, he does offer her name earlier in his book, within a complimentary section that focuses on her maternal qualities as a leader, yet he narrates her death in that section before she serves a storytelling function with Cædmon. In Bede's text, she is resurrected, in a way, to enable the transformation of the first English poet.[11]

Her name was Hilda. She both assented to the truth of Cædmon's wild story, and in inviting him into the monastery to continue crafting religious poems, became his patron. A nun did not write the first English poem, but nuns and sisters have been inextricable from the writing, reading, and sharing of verse for over a thousand years. Levertov was right: they, like the previously silent Cædmon, had been "pulled" into "the ring of the dance" of poetry.[12]

* * *

Gerard Manley Hopkins is the prototypical poet-priest. His pedigree is formidable: an Oxford graduate who was mentored by Cardinal Henry Newman, his conversion to Catholicism made his poetry especially charged with the grandeur of God. His death at forty-four years old left an unfinished life; his reluctance to publish during his lifetime means that his oeuvre forever glows with mystery and promise.

Hopkins's verse was uncannily novel: his lines read like spontaneous bursts of Christological wonder. His notebooks teem with original—and patently genius—observations about the natural world. His prosody feels at once condensed and malleable. Some of his work appears obtuse at first glance, but much like Scripture, contemplation and consideration of these lines reveal hidden gifts. He is often framed as Hopkins the *Jesuit*, with the recognition that the Society of Jesus has created a dizzying number of writers, scholars, lawyers, astronomers, and more.

Hopkins was a poetic anomaly, a man out-of-time, whose work feels technically and spiritually radical even in our contemporary world. He is, in short, a dangerous precedent for writers of religious orders—and perhaps an impossible precedent for women poets of religious orders, who, due to cultural perceptions and institutional restrictions, typically lack the power and autonomy of their male colleagues, even in contemporary times.

Yet like Cædmon, Hopkins would not have been a poet were it not for nuns.

In December 1875, Hopkins was studying theology at St. Beuno's College in Wales. He was deeply drawn to the Welsh language, steeped in vowels that "run off the tongue like oil."[13] He wrote often to his mother, who had sent him clippings of a recent disaster at sea: the *Deutschland*, a German emigrant ship bound for New York City, had wrecked during a terrible storm. More than fifty died, including five Franciscan nuns—who drowned as water filled the ship.

The breathless newspaper reports shook Hopkins. Seven years earlier, when he became a Jesuit novice, Hopkins had famously burned his early poems. What actually rested there as ash is less important than the symbolism: the poet had been reborn, through fire, as a priest. Following the pyre, Hopkins "resolved to write no more, as not belonging to my profession, unless it were by the wish of my superiors."[14] Yet one of those superiors, Father James Jones, SJ, the rector at St. Beuno, noticed how the shipwreck had affected Hopkins. By Christmas Eve of 1875, Hopkins was already "writing something on this wreck"; the tragedy "made a deep impression on me, more than any other wreck or accident I ever read of."[15]

During the seven years of his self-imposed poetic silence, Hopkins had only dabbled in private, short pieces, and a comic poem written for his fellow Jesuits at the college. Yet now, with the tacit encouragement of his rector, and likely buoyed by the fact that the brave nuns were fleeing the anti-Catholic Falk Laws of Germany, Hopkins dove into what he would describe as an "ode."[16]

The poem is invoked to the "happy memory" of these nuns, a phrase rendering his view of them as martyrs. The poem's first stanza reads as Hopkins's formation anew as a poet. He speaks to God, "giver of breath and bread," the "Lord of living and dead."[17] God has "bound bones and veins in me, fastened me flesh," and that body feels God's reminding touch. The poem's second part shifts to a dramatization of the shipwreck: "Into the snows she sweeps"[18] until "night drew her Dead to the Kentish Knock."[19]

With details gleaned from newspaper accounts and his own poetic flourishes, Hopkins captures the violent event: the wailing and crying of passengers amidst the stormy tumult. The nuns had been "Banned by the land of their birth, / Rhine refused them. Thames would ruin them."[20] In contrast, Hopkins-as-speaker laments: "Away in the lovable west, / On a pastoral forehead of Wales, / I was under a roof here, I was at rest, / And they the prey of the gales."[21] His lament is anchored in the recognition that those who suffered and died were sisters in Christ. Although Hopkins was not with them in that storm, he was with them among the lines of the poem—the poetic art that he had stayed away from for so long, and that was the core of his soul. In "The Wreck of the Deutschland," Hopkins the poet-speaker subsumes into the identities of the nuns. Their personae transcend the event itself, and become lives of Christ. Hopkins's first true poem in seven years was a transfiguring act. He finally, truly became a poet by, poetically, taking on the experiences of nuns.

* * *

"Being a sister is rather like the circus feat of riding two horses at once," wrote Sister Maria del Rey, a Maryknoll Sister, in 1964. "The trick is to keep one's feet planted firmly on each animal, but at the same time allow for slips and starts and individual differences."[22] She was living by her own advice: at fifty-seven years old, she was enrolled in Columbia University's Graduate School of Journalism. After receiving her undergraduate degree from the University of Pittsburgh, she worked as a reporter for eight years in the city before entering the Maryknoll Sisters in 1933. She spent three years in a Philippines prison camp during World War II; once back in the United States, she created the order's publicity department. "If the church does not carry on intelligently in this communications field," she affirmed, "its influence on people is going to be negligible."[23]

"Estudia, arguye e enseña, / y es de la Iglesia servicio, / que no la quiere ignorante / El que racional la hizo"; "It is of service to the Church / that women argue, tutor, learn, / for He Who granted women reason / would not have them uninformed."[24] Those lines sound like a rallying cry for modern women of faith like Sister Maria del Rey, but they were written nearly 325 years ago for the matins on a feast of St. Catherine of Alexandria in New Spain, by a nun. That nun was Sor Juana Inés de la Cruz, the daughter of unwed, poor parents: a Creole mother and a Spanish father.

Sor Juana's literary depth and breadth would be the envy of any modern writer. She composed devotional verse and secular love poems, comedies and plays, theological essays and autobiographical treatises, and *villancicos*—liturgical hymns. To say she is without equal is not simply to acknowledge her unique pedigree. One of her biographers, the great Mexican poet Octavio Paz, said Sor Juana was one of the major female poets of the American hemisphere, along with Emily

Dickinson, Gabriela Mistral, Marianne Moore, and Elizabeth Bishop, and concluded Sor Juana is the most distinct.[25]

In 1669, barely out of her teens, Sor Juana professed her vows in the Hieronymite Convent of St. Paula in Mexico City. A gifted child, she had always yearned for knowledge, and the cloistered life seemed a perfect match for a life of learning: "my wish to live alone, to have no fixed occupation which might curtail my freedom of study, nor the noise of a community to interfere with the tranquil stillness of my books."[26] She was entirely self-taught. Our modern sense might think Sor Juana was merely secular, but it is important to remember that she found the origin of her thirst for knowledge was divine. She invoked Mary to talk about reason and wisdom: "Queen of light ... since you illumine the heavens with your splendor ... send us a ray of this divine Light to enlighten our understanding, so that freed from the darkness of human ignorance, we may contemplate heavenly things."[27] In order to reach the "eminence of sacred theology" she had to "ascend the steps of human arts and sciences."[28] She studied rhetoric to discern the "figures, tropes, and locutions" of Holy Scripture. She studied mathematics to understand the computations of Daniel and measurements of proportion of the sacred Ark of the Covenant and Jerusalem.

This sense of divine origin and goal suffused all spheres of her study. When she was medically unable to read for some time, Sor Juana arrived at an epiphany: "Although I did not study in books, I directed my study to all the things God has made. They became my letters, and my book was the machinery of the universe. There was nothing I saw that I did not reflect upon. There was nothing I heard that I did not ponder, even the smallest and most material of things. Because there is no creature, no matter how lowly, in which the *me fecit Deus* [God made me] cannot be found."

Her manner of study was feverish and full. "Blessed be God," she reflected, "for his will to direct [my inclination] toward learning, and not toward some vice or other that would have proved all but irresistible to me."[29] Yet for all of Juana's brilliance and ambition, she was still a woman in the seventeenth century, and she paraphrased the biting criticism of her intellect from her peers and superiors as thus: "This study is incompatible with the blessed ignorance to which you are bound. You will lose your way, at such heights your head will be turned by your very perspicacity and sharpness of mind."[30]

Hundreds of years later, we might still consider Juana Inés de la Cruz the poet laureate of a particular tension: a woman religious writer who wishes to bring the ineffable to secular ears. Juana used literature and poetry as forms of protest and affirmation of her identity. She created a precedent for modern women writers to develop, rather than stifle, the tension between faith and doubt, allegiance and independence. Contemporary readers are often intrigued by the striking modernity of her voice, and challenged by her interweaving of tradition with individuality.

Until the late 1680s, Marqués de la Laguna, the viceroy of New Spain, and his wife María Luisa, Countess of Paredes, afforded Juana significant literary and political freedom, and had her works published in Spain. The convent held a generous library, and was also what Octavio Paz considered a "salon" for intellectuals from, or who visited, Mexico City.[31]

Despite the positive literary elements of her circumstance, Juana remained a radical, perhaps intellectually dangerous voice. She refused deference to masculine tradition, literary or otherwise. "You foolish men who lay / the guilt on women," one poem begins, "not seeing you're the cause / of the very thing you blame." Her metaphors are fresh and clever, her points stinging and true: "What kind of mind is odder / than his who mists / a mirror and then complains / that it's not clear."[32] It is disheartening that many of Sor Juana's radical defenses of women and learning still resound now, hundreds of years later: "Like men, do [women] not have a rational soul? Why then shall they not enjoy the privilege of the enlightenment of letters? Is a woman's soul not as receptive to God's grace and glory as a man's?"[33]

These tensions found their ultimate test in perhaps the most infamous incident in Sor Juana's storied life. In 1690, a critique that she had written of a Portuguese Jesuit's sermon was found and published—without her permission—by the Bishop of Puebla. Adopting the fictional persona of a nun, the bishop wrote a scathing admonition of Sor Juana. That controversy led to Sor Juana's influential and seminal text, the 1691 work *Response to Sor Philotea de la Cruz*. Hailed now by religious and secular feminist critics, the work was the evolution of her rise as an independent voice. Gillian T. W. Ahlgren describes the response as a "carefully reasoned and passionate argument for women's equality but also as a scripturally based rationale for a theological anthropology that assumes women's authority as spiritual and theological teachers." Ahlgren praises even the method of the work, which "invites the reader into the very process of theology itself—a process of reflection, contemplation, debate, and ongoing refinement."[34]

In her time, Sor Juana was known as the "tenth muse," equal to the nine goddesses or muses of antiquity.[35] Yet she largely disappeared from public literary view following the conflict with her bishop. While some biographers have thought she merely began the process of reaffirming or renewing her vows at this time, there is certainly a steep decline in her literary production until her death several years later.

Sor Juana is in no way forgotten, particularly in her native Mexico, where her face appears on the 100-peso bill, and she has been the subject of numerous critical and creative studies, films, and even a television series in early 2016. Sor Juana truly earned the moniker of "First Feminist of the New World." The lines she wrote for the Feast of the Assumption in 1676 perfectly describe her own identity: "Clear the way for the entrance / of the bold adventuress / who undoes injustice / who smashes insults."[36]

* * *

A seventh-century abbess who helped a cowherd turn into a devotional poet, creating a mythic inspiration for generations of storytellers. A nineteenth-century British Jesuit priest whose verse transcends the work of peers and still holds the esteem of contemporary poets. A seventeenth-century sister whose groundbreaking work offers a template for the future.

Abbess Hilda, Gerard Manley Hopkins, and Sor Juana Inés de la Cruz can help us understand the unique alchemy of twentieth-century nun and sister poets. One was a material patron of the arts; her grace and wisdom cultivated an obscure talent—and created a mythos. One was a poet of the highest order who demonstrated that a writer of great piety could serve as a model of dynamic prosody. One was a trailblazing nun whose brilliance and skill are a template for modern writers.

The Habit of Poetry: The Literary Lives of Nuns in Mid-century America will reveal how a group of nuns and sisters, in their own diverse ways, synthesized these creative and critical concerns. Their literary predecessors were formidable; those grand shadows could appear overwhelming. Yet for the women portrayed in this book, poetry was the language of their hearts and minds, and the most perfect way to ponder belief and doubt. Much like Cædmon, they retreated from the wider, bustling world—and sometimes retreated from the communities of their convents and institutions—to discover the song of poetry. Their inspirations varied, and their styles differed, yet they shared a deep concern for the place of an individual woman within a larger order. The legacy of these mid-century nun and sister poets is notable: that in an increasingly secular world, skilled and inspired work from religious poets can still shine, even as those poets wrestle with their identities and faith.

ACKNOWLEDGMENTS

Sections of this book previously appeared in different forms in *America*, *Literary Hub*, *National Review*, and *US Catholic*. I appreciate the support of those editors.

Gratitude to my parents and family. Many thanks to my editor, Emily King, and the entire team at Fortress Press.

Love and heartfelt appreciation to Jennifer, Amelia, and Olivia. You inspired me to write this book!

INTRODUCTION

Sister Mary Madeleva Wolff: Measured Ambition

ANTS HUDDLED IN the center of the cover for the Winter 1960–61 issue of *Poetry Northwest*, a quarterly literary magazine published in Seattle, Washington. The cover art was taken from "Ant War," a painting by Oregon-born artist Morris Graves. Although based in the Pacific Northwest, the magazine's writers and artists hailed from the region, and beyond. Founded the previous year, the magazine had already published Anne Sexton, Stanley Kunitz, and Philip Larkin. In this issue alone, luminaries like William Stafford, Donald Hall, Thom Gunn, and Philip Levine published alongside lesser-known writers like Allyn Wood and Sister Mary Gilbert, a Sister of the Holy Names of Jesus and Mary.

The issue featured three poems by Gilbert, born Madeline DeFrees, who taught at Holy Names College in Spokane, Washington. The editors called her "one of a lively and generously gifted group of young Catholic poets."[1] "Tumbleweed" ponders the "mobile American par excellence," and appreciates how "rootlessness" is "its survival."[2] In "A Kind of Resurrection," Gilbert deftly paces single-sentence stanzas. Yet the strongest poem of the trio is both timely and instructive. "Nuns in the Quarterlies" at first appears niche—but reveals much about mid-century nun-poets.

Gilbert begins by documenting how nuns often appear in art: "Used as accents in a landscape or seaview, / upright in merciful black on the sand's monotone, / not even the devil's advocate could question / their purely decorative purpose."[3] These nuns are calming: "they are all suggestion, / posing no problem deeper than the eye."[4]

Elsewhere in culture, nuns are depicted in more unusual ways: "an evening frolic / through slicker pages of the thicker magazines

/ where nuns drift in and out of nightmare scenes." Nuns perfectly encapsulate female archetypes: "Women, the ancient lie, the unattainable mystery, / the apple high on paradisal branches, / the history of heaven and hell, of fall and pardon; / innocence unmasked in God's own Garden."[5] Gilbert ends with an affirmation: "Nuns are the fictions / by whom we verify the usual contradictions."[6]

The poem is light but not loose; perceptive but not taciturn. Its points are well taken, and yet it seems composed with a wink. Sister Mary Gilbert was a nun, and she was in the quarterlies. Her poem catalogs stereotypical presentations of nuns, but doesn't address the nuanced skill of her own work: the poetry of a nun. She wasn't alone: in mid-twentieth-century America, nuns were publishing widely in the finest literary publications. Something, it seems, was happening— and it is time we understand why these nuns were drawn to writing and publishing poetry. Perhaps nuns could be their most artistic and authentic selves among these pages; their measured and skilled lines suggest literary and personal ambitions that can help illuminate the religious lives of women of their time.

* * *

By 1930, Ezra Pound's life was inextricable from literary magazines. His poetry and prose regularly appeared in *Poetry*, *New Age*, *Little Review*, and *The Egoist*. As an editor, he arranged for the serialization of two Modernist classics in magazines: *A Portrait of the Artist as a Young Man* and *Ulysses*, both by James Joyce.

Pound alternately referred to these magazines as "small," "little," "impractical," and "fugitive periodicals."[7] In addition to Joyce, Pound cites William Carlos Williams, Marianne Moore, Wallace Stevens, Ernest Hemingway, T. S. Eliot, and H. D. as essential writers who were formed by, and continued to publish in, literary magazines. Commercial magazines, Pound lamented, "have been content and are still more than content to take derivative products ten or twenty years after the germ has appeared in the free magazines."[8]

The great work of any period is formed not in sleek, widely distributed pages, but in literary magazines: "The work of writers who have emerged in or via such magazines outweighs in permanent value the work of the writers who have not emerged in this manner. The history of contemporary letters has, to a very manifest extent, been written in such magazines."[9] The most effective literary magazines, argues Pound, publish not only poetry and fiction, but also criticism—recognizing that criticism sustains creative work.

Pound knew that literary magazines often died young. No matter. The "active periodical" is a risk worth taking; the best magazine "definitely, even with foolhardiness, asserts its hope and ambition."[10] These magazines built literature from the ground up, in America and abroad.

Pound's argument doesn't only apply to the Modernist literary magazine. Writing in 1962—the time when the nuns and sisters of *The Habit of Poetry* were a force in American literary magazines—librarian and poet Felix Pollak attempted to describe the "spirit" of these magazines. Their "essence" was one of "wide-openness and receptivity to new ideas, theories, movements, and experiments; a stubborn refusal to conform to conventions and mores; an air of independence, a fervid antagonism against fetters and trammels and chains and strings of any kind; a stance of active resistance against the theory and practice of censorship and taboo." Unlike large commercial magazines, "bound to advertising interests and circulation figures," literary magazines have a spirit that "is free and gay and irreverent and deadly earnest and intense, pugnacious and ebullient, often irresponsible, always irrepressible."[11]

Pollak tempers his romantic sense of literary magazines by affirming their lack of traditional utility: "the little magazines will fulfill their basic function of providing catacombs for minority tastes and values: they are the fallout shelters against mass-minded vulgarity." These magazines reflected the culture of the moment in sharp, often paradoxical ways, and were a place for experimentation, including the occasional "failure."[12]

Literary magazines were places for emerging voices to publish alongside established, award-winning writers. The magazines were read by ambitious writers, and resulted in a self-sustaining literary economy. These magazines, along with select, larger publications with notable critical sections, were spaces for the cultivation of original work, but also places for debate and reflection.

One magazine that curated an especially robust conversation about American literature was published by Philadelphia's La Salle College, founded by the Christian Brothers. *Four Quarters* debuted in 1951, and included several brothers on the masthead. The quarterly affirmed it was "aimed at focusing the practice and appreciation of writing in the Catholic tradition."[13] The magazine regularly published poetry by priests, brothers, and nuns.

The June 1955 issue included a symposium titled "Does American Catholic Education Produce Its Share of Leaders in the Literary Field?" The symposium operated from the position that there was a "dearth of top-rank Catholic literary leaders from Catholic colleges and universities."[14] The magazine then solicited reactions for future issues from "authors, teachers, and literary critics" in response to a pointed question: why don't "Catholic colleges and universities in the United States . . . produce an adequate supply of Catholic writers?"[15]

Respondents included the poet Allen Tate, a Catholic convert, who took a pessimistic yet realistic view. Other than James Joyce and Marcel Proust, he claimed, the "great discoveries of modern literature" have "been made by non-Catholics." The Catholic intellectual, he lamented, "is oppressed by a consciousness of belonging to a minority."[16] The playwright Arthur Miller prefaced his comments with a confession: "I have never stepped inside a Catholic college." Writing, he explained, "is a heartbreakingly difficult thing to do well principally because the truth is so difficult to know, even under the best circumstances." He imagined that if such writing "is in part hedged about with fears and warnings against transgression of dogma, it obviously makes writing even more difficult."[17]

The final word went to a Sister Mary Madeleva Wolff, who asserted the "paucity of creative writers in our Catholic colleges is only a fraction of the general impoverishment in creative writing from which we are suffering everywhere." Writers need time, and the right conditions, to create—both of which, she thought, were in short supply. "A thunder storm can addle a whole nest of eggs under a setting hen and kill the embryonic chicks," she noted. "Can you think what the tumultuous situations of our past quarter of a century have effected in the possible creative thought of possible writers?"[18] What was needed, Sister Madeleva argued, was "patient, tireless hard work, careful, thoughtful reading selected with fastidious care, an intolerance of mediocrity in one's self are all parts of the process."

She concluded: "There are no easy ways."[19]

* * *

"Modern poets are talking about their digestive systems, their empty skulls, and of the refuse of humanity."[20] Quite the literary jab in 1962—from a nun, no less. Yet Sister Mary Madeleva Wolff, CSC (1887–1964), was not speaking from the sidelines; she was a poet herself, whose *Collected Poems* were praised by the *New York Times* as having "melodic skill." Despite the poems' "orthodox piety," the reviewer wrote, her "appeal is a popular one."[21]

Best known for administrative accomplishments—she served as president of Saint Mary's College, Notre Dame for twenty-seven years and founded the School of Sacred Theology, the first graduate theology school for lay persons, in 1943—Sister Madeleva Wolff was a dedicated poet. She studied medieval literature at Oxford with C. S. Lewis and J. R. R. Tolkien, and earned her PhD in English from the University of California at Berkeley. "I wrote at least one poem a month over a period of 15 or 20 years, every one of which I sent out at once to earn its living by publication in some magazine," Wolff said, her work appearing in *The New Republic, Commonweal,* and the *New York Times,* among others.[22]

She corresponded with Thomas Merton, a mutual admirer, for fifteen years—although she could be blunt in her criticism of his work: "It takes a whole field of flowers to make a gram of perfume."[23] Wolff was a singular figure, steeled by wit and faith, but she was not alone in her poetic prowess. Her life is a window into a mid-century renaissance of nun-poets. The work of these poets is more than a literary footnote: it is a case study in how women negotiate tradition and individual creativity.

* * *

"You hold me only when you set me free." When asked by *Life* magazine—which featured a profile of her in the June 10, 1957, issue—how she approached discipline in her all-women's college, Wolff said her method was "the relaxed grasp."[24] She then quoted the clever line from one of her own poems, capturing the paradoxes of religious life. Wolff was a sister for most of her life, but her structured existence was not stricture, but source.

Wolff was born on May 24, 1887, in Cumberland, Wisconsin, a roughly two-mile-long island in Beaver Dam Lake, which she called "one of the deep loves of my life."[25] She ran between, and sometimes climbed, the lumber stacks that piled around the mill town. Railway development to the island led to an influx of immigrants, and parts of Mass were soon spoken in English, French, German, and Italian.[26]

Far from any Catholic schools, Wolff had a public education. She loved to read, but was neither drawn to her English teachers nor the subject itself in school. Her first attempt at poetry was a short translation of Johann Wolfgang von Goethe within her high school commencement essay in June 1904. She attended the University of Wisconsin, and enjoyed her first year there. She spent summer break home with her old "crowd": "We talked, danced, swam, motored by land and water...We came home bronzed with tan and starved for sleep."[27]

Amidst that summer fun, though, Wolff longed for something more. She noticed an advertisement for Saint Mary's College in Notre Dame, Indiana, an all-women's Catholic school. She transferred, and the decision began her journey as both a nun and a poet, as the two identities were later inextricable from each other. Wolff was drawn to Sister Rita Heffernan, a Harvard-educated professor who would go on European trips with Elizabeth Jordan, the editor of *Harper's Bazaar*.[28] Sister Rita assigned a lyric verse project, but Wolff was nervous. She felt that she couldn't write original poetry, and ultimately translated more Goethe. The attempt at original work, despite the struggle, stirred Wolff. "I had come upon a manner of writing that I had never tried or been taught to use before," she reflected. "The discovery exhilarated me. After that I would lie awake at night trying to fashion every lovely thing I knew into verse. I had found my medium."[29]

Her religious devotion came next. An independent spirit from her public school days, Wolff eschewed the college's rules. Some days she would skip class and instead go outside; when pressed by the school's prefect, Wolff was curt: "Sister, some of the rules, I think, are rather foolish."[30] She changed her perspective, though, after a religious retreat, when she concluded "the religious life was what I most desired and for which I had most completely disqualified myself. God did not make sisters out of girls like me."[31] Yet she had been changed for good: "I will do anything that God wants me to, if I can only find out what it is."[32]

After her second year at Saint Mary's, Wolff made a decision. Despite doubts that a young woman such as herself could become a sister, she felt compelled to pursue a religious vocation, and decided to become a Sister of the Holy Cross. Originally founded in France in 1841, the congregation soon moved to Notre Dame, establishing Saint Mary's College. Wolff entered the congregation on September 14, 1908, and on December 10 received her habit, and the name of Sister Mary Madeleva.[33] During the next decade, she taught literature, theology, and philosophy at the university, but never forgot how poetry had captivated her. She enrolled in a Master's program in literature at Notre Dame, and was heartened that her professor thought one of her sonnets was worthy of publication. Wolff made a promise to herself:

> *Two rules I set for myself at the very beginning. I would publish under my religious name. I would submit my work first to secular rather than to Catholic magazines. I had heard so much about Catholics being unable to receive recognition because they were Catholics. I resolved not to permit mediocrity in my writing to be attributed to my religion. As a Catholic and a sister I would write well enough for acceptance by the secular press, or I would not write at all.*[34]

* * *

Wolff's *ars poetica* is a fitting manifesto for *The Habit of Poetry*. A nun or priest who consistently publishes verse is a novelty. It is notable that these members of religious orders participated within the insular, narrow world of American letters, including literary magazines. The average twentieth-century reader of literature, one who read books, did not likely have much encounter with literary magazines.

Yet those readers were intimately aware of the *writers* who published in those magazines. A 1955 advertisement for *Renascence*, "a quarterly review to promote literary criticism and to evaluate contemporary literature," includes a short list of recent contributors: luminaries including W. H. Auden, Thomas Merton, J. F. Powers, Graham Greene, Marshall McLuhan, and Sister Madeleva.[35] Mid-century issues of *The Kenyon Review* included a nearly dizzying array of contributors: Flannery O'Connor, Robert Penn Warren, Dylan Thomas, Robert Lowell, Thomas Pynchon, T. S. Eliot, Nadine Gordimer, John Barth, Jean Stafford, William Carlos Williams, and others.

Taking a broader view of the phenomenon in 1962, Felix Pollak asserted that about "80 per cent of the serious writers in this century . . . were first published in the littles," another term for literary magazines. These writers, though, did not use literary magazines as publishing stepping stones; "they are not the kindergartens of literature, and genuine avant-garde writers, particularly those who continued to grow and venture, kept appearing in them long after they had gained renown and even fame."[36] Literary magazines, with their regular publication schedule and level of respect among readers and writers in the publishing world, both helped writers like James Joyce, Ezra Pound, William Faulkner, Ernest Hemingway, and Gertrude Stein develop, and "*speeded* their rise."[37] The most generous interpretation, then, is that literary magazines are the "furnace where contemporary literature is being forged"—an industrial metaphor that nicely matches the workshop-lingo of the creative writing classroom.[38] A more conservative interpretation is still complimentary: even if the literature itself is forged elsewhere, "what little magazines do is affirm that the written imagination matters."[39]

It was into this literary world that Wolff ventured with her poems, making regular appearances in their pages as she continued her education beyond Notre Dame at Cal Berkeley and Oxford, and began to collect her poems into published books. "I know of no discipline more merciless, more demanding than the writing of good verse," Wolff wrote, her choice of "discipline" an allusion to her complex identity beyond the page.[40] In one of her scholarly examinations of Geoffrey Chaucer, Wolff considered the transformation of self that occurred when a woman becomes a nun or sister: "a woman whose life has undergone a change more subtle and entirely spiritual than marriage but quite as real...The forces by which this change is effected are two: the first, a mystical but most real relation between the soul and God; the second, the rules and customs and religious practices of the particular community in which the individual seeks to perfect that mystical relation."[41]

Wolff was fond of saying that "poetry is thousands of years older than soap," an affirmation that hers was an ancient art, essential to the human spirit.[42] She also recognized the paradoxes of her identity. She was a formidable public figure: when she quipped "I'm merely a janitor. That's what a college president is," she was being coy to *Life* magazine, but knew that her poetry life was a private, internal one.[43] "Poetry I think of as a distillation requiring undistracted time in large quantities. This no sister that I know of has ever had," Wolff lamented, while affirming that the "religious life is the model school in resourcefulness."[44] Without the leisure of undisturbed time, Wolff "found myself isolating thoughts, husbanding moments walking to and from class, holding every fraction of quiet for milling these thoughts into lyric form. The process has been continuous and almost more secret than my conscience."[45]

Wolff wrote that the "religious rule of silence was my best work-shop."[46] Although she exchanged poetry manuscripts with her friend Father Charles O'Donnell and such esteemed poets as Joyce Kilmer (during her early years as a poet), her craft unfolded mostly in silence, much like prayer. In fact, later in life, she wrote to her religious superior that poetry was a "means of sanctification for me," and that "much of it is prayer to me."[47]

Poetry was a necessary stay against the confusion, and stress, of her administrative life. "The impact of prosaic demands is all but fatal to lyric thinking and expression," she wrote in 1950.[48] The next year she made similar complaints in a letter to C. S. Lewis: "The impact of administration for these past seventeen years has been desolating so far as adventures in thinking are concerned."[49] Publicly, though, she was more democratic in the descriptions of her labor—"in addition to my executive duties I am a teacher, chaperone, match-maker, hiker"—while still voicing her great lament: "I regret that I haven't more time, because the ideas I have for poetry—and I believe it is the same with all of us—simply haunt me until I can get them out of my system. And, believe me, it takes hard work and a lot of discomfort to write poetry. It has to hurt you a lot."[50]

Despite the lack of time to focus her thoughts, Wolff was preternaturally drawn to verse. Her identity as a poet was not merely an artistic identity, but also a *spiritual* one. Wolff thought that poets of faith see "in human beings a reflection of God. He looks out upon a transfigured, supernaturalized landscape, an immortalized vision of life."[51] Modern secular poets, unfortunately, caused "emetic ecstasy." She said those poets "lack faith and hope. They accuse others of being escapists, not realistic. Actually they are running away from the beauty and truth that is perennial."[52] Fiction, she thought, fared even worse. Readers of contemporary novels are unfortunately "wallowing in garbage" because artists "have eliminated all the moral considerations. We believe that accepting a moral obligation in any area is intruding upon our personal freedoms and therefore we must not be inhibited by the ideas of right and wrong. We must be unrestrained in our actions and in our thinking."[53]

Armed with a pugilistic literary sense, Wolff broke through into spaces that were typically reserved for men. Beyond the largely male contributor lists of contemporary literary magazines, she also gained a reputation for being a lively speaker. During the 1957–58 academic year, Boston College ran the David B. Steinman Visiting Poets Series, which included Robert Frost, Ogden Nash, T. S. Eliot, and Sister Madeleva, the only woman invited to speak.[54]

In order to understand Wolff's unique identity as a woman religious who excelled in the largely male spaces of academia and literature, we might again consider her scholarly work on Chaucer. Writing of Chaucer's prioress, she says: "But here is his picture of a woman a decade or more beyond middle age (my opinion) sweetened and spiritually transformed by the rules and religious practices of her choice, who can be in the world without being of it, gracious without affection, and friendly without boldness."[55] The prioress, Wolff observes, "combines the wisdom of the serpent with the simplicity of the dove."[56]

Wise and deft herself, Wolff reached the status of an icon. Reflecting on her life several decades after her death, Father John W. Donohue, SJ, was laudatory: "During the three decades before the Second Vatican Council she was the best-known Catholic sister in the United States—the nun as a diva in her fluted wimple and flowing veil."[57] Elsewhere she was described as "probably the best-known nun in the world."[58] She was likely the inspiration for Ingrid Bergman's character in *The Bells of Saint Mary's*.[59] She spent time with W. B. Yeats, G. K. Chesterton, Jacques Maritain, and other influential writers, who were drawn to her wit and poetic sense. She was, for a time, the president of the Catholic Poetry Society of America. Her poem "Snow Storm" was featured at the 1939 New York World's Fair. As writers like Garry Wills would reflect, "she was an important person in the Catholic schools of my youth, a great source of pride and morale since she proved that a nun could be a scholar (Ph.D., Berkeley), a prize-winning poet, and a community leader (vice president of the Indiana Conference of Higher Education)."[60] Wolff had accomplished her ambitious goal as a young poet: "Having laid the ghost of rampant discrimination against Catholic writers I got into my own Church and my own pew."[61] She was, as *Life* magazine wrote, "a nun with no nonsense about her."[62] She had great ambition for her verse—and for her fellow nuns.

* * *

During the 1948 meeting of the National Catholic Educational Association, Wolff, then president of Saint Mary's College in Indiana, called for comprehensive reform of how Catholic school teachers were prepared, particularly nuns and sisters. Wolff addressed criticisms of Catholic education: "with inadequate plans and only partially trained teachers for three hundred years, we have been taking care of our young people."[63] The women tasked with this education oftentimes must work from "sheer courage and conviction" rather than adequate economic and pedagogical support.[64] Wolff's complaints followed the observations of Sister Bertrande Myers of the Daughters of Charity, whose doctoral dissertation for Saint Louis University examined how sisters had to parcel their education through summer sessions rather than traditional schooling: "in the majority of cases, the experience seems to have destroyed rather than nurtured any love of learning."[65]

During the 1949 session, Wolff and other presenters on teacher education had to move to a series of larger venues to fit their audience, before they "settled in the gymnasium with people sitting on the steps and in the aisles."[66] Wolff's own speech, "The Education of Sister Lucy," described the hypothetical Lucy Young, a recent high school graduate who becomes a novitiate with the goal of becoming a teacher. Her "two trainings are completely compatible, complementary, and can be perfectly synchronized."[67] She pursues a rigorous college education, and only once she makes her final vows can "she begin at once to carry on the work to which she is dedicated."[68]

"I need not tell you that Sister Lucy does not exist," Wolff acknowledges. "But I know that we all should insist that she shall exist. We are here in part to bring her into existence."[69] Wolff rejects concerns about money. "If we cannot afford to prepare our young sisters for the work of our communities, we should not accept them at all," while also noting: "the material in our habits is some of the most expensive cloth made. We argue that it wears a long time. So does education. If we can afford to clothe Lucy's body, we can also afford to clothe her mind."[70]

The work of that session ultimately bore fruit in August 1952, when the Sister Formation Conference held its first national congress. The Sister Formation Movement was not without its detractors, notably those who feared a more extensive formation program for teaching sisters "would delay the number of teachers available for expanding parochial schools."[71] Sister Maura Eichner, a fellow poet, lauded the program's "broad intellectual as well as spiritual and professional training."[72] Like other women featured in *The Habit of Poetry*, Eichner's professional and creative lives were inextricable; her work was an affirmation that she, like the other women of her time, was to be taken seriously.

Sister Madeleva had certainly earned a high level of respect in the literary world. In 1960, five years after their previous symposium,

Four Quarters again invited Wolff to contribute her thoughts to a debate on the teaching of creative writing. Organized by Brother Felician Patrick, FSC, participants included Ray Bradbury, Flannery O'Connor, John O'Hara, James Michener, Katherine Anne Porter, and John F. Kennedy—perhaps the only president-elect to appear in a literary magazine.

"We need a creative America today," Kennedy argued. Creativity means new ideas and leadership; otherwise, a people can only be enslaved: "They have no vision, no imagination to beckon them, no direction in which to move."[73] The ultimate goal of a creative writing program, as well as other visionary fields, was to synthesize "craftsmanship and creativeness."[74]

Sister Madeleva, imbued with the rhetorical flair of a politician but anchored in the reality of pastoral life, offered a different response. "If creative writing can be taught, novelists, dramatists, poets should be, or could be, as numerous as engineers, scientists, teachers, experts in our various professional fields," she wrote. "The fact that they are not, implies a qualification or a condition or both essential to creative writing and apart from the most excellent instruction." This "distinct gift" is not teachable, but that does not eliminate the worth of sustained writing instruction. The best teachers create "an atmosphere of creative aptitude, stimulation, encouragement, companionship."

The goal of creative writing instruction, for Sister Madeleva, was not to create a legion of professional writers. Students will leave those courses "with a new sense of wonder in the use of words," which, after all, is the "validity of such study; in the beginning was the Word and for all eternity, the Word is God."[75]

*   *   *

Of the women portrayed in *The Habit of Poetry*, Sister Madeleva Wolff wrote the most traditional verse. Her work does not contain the melancholy style of Jessica Powers, or the experimental turns of Sister Maura Eichner. We should remember her context, though: while she was certainly not the first woman religious to publish poetry in America, she was perhaps the earliest to consistently do so in secular literary magazines and publications, while also reaching a popular audience. Thomas Merton felt that he and other members of religious orders were able to publish in secular venues because of her precedent.[76]

She also offered a precedent for American writers of religious orders to speak about poetry as a worthwhile, spiritual identity, one that can refigure our sense of bodies. In a 1958 speech, Wolff separated her project from the work of philosophy. The poet, she noted, "is not an authority on truth." Rather, the poet's goal is "to take truth from the philosopher and fashion it into a jewel to set it in a form of beauty."[77] The poetic process is one of transformation, with the ultimate goal to make the abstract more aesthetic.

Later in her speech, she offers an inspiring theology of the body. She speaks of how "our bodies are decried as miserable and sinful, and the occasion of a great many disorders, and we blame them for all sorts of inordinate appetites and desires and uncontrolled feelings." Her religious audience knows that her words are an indictment of their own community: of believers who vilify the body. Wolff thinks, though, that we are unfair to our bodies. God, she reminds them, "has shown many preferences for bodies. He has given them to us, has created them. He accepted a body Himself, through the natural means of birth." The sacraments, she reminds her audience, are the ways in which God ministers "to our souls through the avenues of the body," a grace not even given to the angels. Finally, "God has promised that our bodies shall be restored at the end of time and will be glorified and immortal. Now, that is quite a good deal for these miserable bodies."[78]

Wolff pushed her own body to the limit. Her breakneck work as a pioneering university administrator and her travels likely contributed to her chronic illness. The paradox of the body as a source of frailty and wonder, and the constant presence of death, is the anchor of her verse. In the titular poem from her 1923 debut, *Knights Errant and Other Poems*, she writes: "Death is no foreman, we were born together; / He dwells between the places of my breath."[79] Poems like "Sister Death" are direct in their memento mori, while others, like the brief "Wind Wraith," whisper a melancholy awareness of mortality: "A shy ghost of a wind was out / Tiptoeing through the air / At dawn, and though I could not see / Nor hear her anywhere, / I felt her lips just brush my cheek, / Her fingers touch my hair."[80]

In "Of Wounds," from *A Question of Lovers and Other Poems* (1935), Wolff imagines how Mary might have encountered the resurrected Christ. "Being His mother, I had wished His body flawless," Mary speaks, "Fearing to think how beautiful might be / Five wounds upon it. / I know now they are as beautiful as God."[81] Wolff even offers contemplation of her own end, as in "Details for My Burial": "There needs but a small grave where I may lie / Cut in the snow's white peace I love so well."[82]

Wolff's ability to write about death across her entire life as a poet certainly arises from her belief that it is from dust that we are, and to which we shall return, but likely also comes from her humor. Great for a sly quote in an article, Wolff's humor was essential to her life as a woman religious. When students asked about the best books to help for writing, she joked "The *Bible*, the *Oxford Dictionary*, seed catalogues."[83] In "Concerning Certain Manners of Dress," from *Penelope and Other Poems* (1927), Wolff titles her first section "Questions on a Nun's Habit," a sardonic nod to the queries she would receive from those outside convent walls. "You do not think it is because I do not share / A woman's subtle weakness for the piquancy of dress, / Its swift, sure coquetry, its studied carelessness," she writes, "That I wear what I wear?"[84] She turns the inquiries against her interrogators: "Of all the dozen gowns I ever wore / And have abandoned, orchid and shadow-gray and powder-blue, / This is the only one that you need envy me. / —You have not ever cared to find me beautiful before, / Have you?"[85] (In her memoir, *My First Seventy Years*, Wolff wryly observed: "I have never seen a religious habit in which I would choose to spend the rest of my life for beauty's sake, spelling beauty with a small b."[86])

Although Wolff wrote her share of devotional verse, she would be the first to admit that "there is no reason, anyway, why a nun should write pious poetry."[87] Perhaps her finest verse is not directly about God. Her most accomplished book, *Four Girls* (1941), stands well against the secular work of its period. In these poems, Wolff creates an internal, recursive profluence to her lines, as with perhaps her most famous poem, "Snow Storm." All but one of the poem's ten lines are endstopped with periods or semicolons, which might seem like a stilted punctuation choice for recursivity, but Wolff's method is sound. The first line is a single sentence: "The air is white and winds are crying." The first clause is a literal, visual description, while the second clause is acoustic and more metaphorical. The sentence arrives as a complete thought, although the poem's second line completes the first: "I think of swans in Galway flying."

The effect is deft; Wolff is able to create a simultaneous yet connected narrative, in which observation and memory are inextricable. The two narratives turn within each other in both syntax and sense, as Wolff's stanzas smoothly reveal: "Winds are birds; snow is a feather; / Wild white swans are wind and weather."[88] The swans, flying against the background of the sky and pushed by wind, become the weather itself. Wolff ends with a stanza that contains her only enjambed line: "Winds are white with snow but alway / Mine are white with swans from Galway."[89]

Wolff was aware, consciously or not, that poetry was uniquely suited to the identity of women religious. In her preface to *The Four Last Things*, her collected poems, she wrote that poetry "is a distillation, not a diffusion; a high concentrate, not an atomizer."[90] She believed that "the cloistered monastery is of all places the most perfect home of the most perfect poetry."[91] It is typical to imagine religious life as suffocating; a place where art goes to die. Wolff complicates that stereotype, and she is not alone.

Religious life is repetitive. Yet within that repetition are the bends and turns of habit which offer quiet revelations. In "The Theme," one of her early poems as a sister, Wolff's narrator speaks to God of her daily prayers, in which she fears she is being repetitive: "Until I fear that Thou must wearied be / To have no other speech than this from me." The narrator imagines God's response: "Do not I / tire of the tireless sun, the constant sky, / The faithful stars forever slipping by?"[92] It is the poet's work to document this world of wonders, tired as we may become of this world's struggles. In the middle of the twentieth century, a group of poets—nuns and sisters, believers and doubters— spoke their truths. As Wolff wrote to the superior of a young nun who wished to share her poetry with the wider world, "I often wonder at the lack of trust we show in these gifts [of God] when they are bestowed within the beautiful security of the cloister."[93] *The Habit of Poetry* reveals how these complex gifts of God transcend that beautiful security, and are worthy of our attention.

1

JESSICA POWERS: PASTORAL MYSTIC

"I SHOULD LIKE to go to New York."[1] Jessica Powers (1905–88) spent the decade following her mother's death in 1925 as a homemaker, tending to the family farmhouse in Mauston, Wisconsin, to support her brothers. With the marriage of her second brother, she was finally free to pursue a literary dream: moving to the urban center of contemporary poetry in America.

Despite the demanding nature of her domestic work, Powers had published more than fifty poems, including work in *Spirit*, the bimonthly magazine of the Catholic Poetry Society.[2] Established in 1931, the society's purpose was the "fostering and developing of further strength in the body of Catholic culture and literature throughout the nation."[3] The society included a number of Jesuit priests, poet Aline Kilmer (the wife of famed poet Joyce Kilmer), and Sister Mary Madeleva Wolff, and was headquartered at the office of *America* magazine in New York City.

Powers finally moved to New York City in 1937. She stayed at the Leo House, a Catholic guesthouse in Chelsea run by the Sisters of St. Agnes, and began attending meetings of the Catholic Poetry Society at the *America* building. Regular attendees at these meetings included John Brunini, editor of *Spirit*, Clifford Laube, suburban editor of the *New York Times*, and Eileen Surles, whose work in publishing would later be traded in for life as a Cenacle Sister. Powers's life, it seems, was suffused with women who would choose to devote their lives to the church.

Although Powers spoke about moving to New York City for religious reasons—"I wanted to lead a more spiritual life," she would say, "I wanted to get closer to spiritual sources"—the city had also become a bit of a Catholic literary hub in recent years.[4] In 1933 alone, the publisher Sheed & Ward had opened an office in the city, and *The Catholic Worker* newspaper debuted. When Powers left the city proper to live in Tuckahoe in Westchester County, New York, she remained under its literary influence. She took care of the children of Jessie Pegis, a fellow member of the Catholic Poetry Society, and Anton Charles Pegis, a Fordham University philosophy professor who examined the religious elements of Powers's poems.[5] Borrowing from their extensive home library, Powers read Gerard Manley Hopkins and G. K. Chesterton, and her childcare duties actually resulted in a blessing: time to write. Her first book, *The Lantern Burns*, was published in 1939, and garnered glowing praise in *America*, which said Powers was in "the front rank of living Catholic poets."[6]

Powers was a rising Catholic writer at a time when Catholics were acutely aware of their tenuous intellectual status in America. Her literary life—and her ultimate decision to leave the secular literary world for a life as a cloistered nun—encapsulates the tensions and aspirations of mid-century nun-poets.

* * *

In December 1935, Myles Connolly was in the early days of a budding film career. After working as an associate producer on several projects, he was now writing films. Soon he would contribute to the screenplay for *Mr. Smith Goes to Washington* and garner an Academy Award nomination for his original screenplay for *Music for Millions*. His career had taken quite the pivot from his earlier literary life, first as the editor of *Columbia*, the magazine of the Knights of Columbus, and then as the author of *Mr. Blue*, an enigmatic, deft 1928 novel about an earnestly Catholic, mysterious former millionaire turned mystic.

A friend and collaborator of Frank Capra, Connolly was focused on the cinematic world, but retained an interest in Catholic literature. Writing for *America* magazine, the national Jesuit weekly where many of the women depicted in *The Habit of Poetry* would often publish, Connolly considered the state of Catholic writing. Wry, Connolly could be by turns caustic and sentimental, his jocular prose unsurprising from a Boston native turned reporter.

In his essay, Connolly writes of going out to dinner with two friends, both Catholic writers, and lamenting how "our talk fell in its catch-breath moments to that dullest and most constant of subjects, the Catholic Writer."[7] He thought the nighttime conversation was breathless and emotional but wanted to take a more objective stab at the discussion in his article. Although "there is no paucity of American Catholic writers appearing in contemporary print,"[8] few of them "are readable."[9] Instead, he concludes, "they constitute a voice that is about as effectual as the crackling of a frosted telephone wire in the depth of night."[10]

He didn't doubt the piety of these Catholic writers but he doubted their literary skill. They have managed to convinced themselves that "truth, however stupidly stated, eventually triumphs."[11] Their dullness comes from a "general captiousness and cantankerousness; secondly, a complete lack of a desire to entertain."[12] These Catholic writers would much rather argue, arising from an "extraordinary sense of inferiority which prompts bragging that someone like Babe Ruth is a Catholic and, at practically the same moment, resenting *any* criticism as unjust and malevolent."[13] This sense of inferiority "comes from a weakness that knows no calm, no subtlety, no ingenuity, a weakness that defends itself with an obvious everlasting chip on the shoulder."[14]

Before one thinks Connolly is spewing an anti-Catholic sentiment that admittedly stained his era, or that he participated in some strange self-hatred, it helps to recognize that American Catholics have always been most critical of our own. Such a tendency is not exclusive to Catholics but is certainly sharpened by the fact that many of us are sons and daughters of immigrants, families for whom the middle class was an aspiration but not often a reality. Connolly's criticism comes from a place of love and brotherhood.

He ends his essay with advice for Catholic writers to reach a wider, more engaged audience. Although he is part of a larger community, ultimately the Catholic writer must practice "rigid individual discipline and preparation." He must "discover and hew to a standard of taste." Essentially, "in the silence of his own soul he must work out his style, which is his salvation."[15]

His description perfectly fits Powers, whose contributions to *America* were appended with the biographical description as "a Milwaukee poet of New York."[16] One poem written in 1939, halfway through her time in New York, captures her emotions and paradoxes. "Morning of Fog" renders sharp, almost blistering juxtapositions. Powers contrasts death and life, night and day, the material and spiritual. The narrator seems emotionally and imagistically torn; her mood in the city is dictated by time and weather. The poem is both a snapshot of her life in its context, and a representation of lifelong tensions.

Cloaked in morning fog, "this city of death with its gray face" is the same place where later her "thoughts stir wild and free." "It is a road I trace / too eagerly," she writes, a nod to the cross streets that map her life in the city, but also a recognition that she invites the varieties of self. Although the poem is static in its setting, the narrator feels itinerant, drawn to another place.

In the second stanza, she again invokes death in her description of morning. "The towers lift / like dreams," she writes, a gentle, nearly heavenly allusion pulled downward with an enigmatic description of how the "beautiful / gray fogs of sorrow drift" back to earth.

Her next line reveals impressive skill. "This is a city of phantoms," she writes, the phrase its own sentence, appended with the enjambed "I am lost." Although she is weary in this place "where nothing that beats with life should / roam," this *is* her home; her purgatory of sorts. When she laments that "Only a spirit chilled into a ghost / could call these streets its home," it is a recognition that she is among those phantoms.

"I shall go exiled to the fall of night," she begins the final stanza, hoping that she can return in the day "to the city I love where the streets are washed with light / and the windows burn."[17]

Four years later, Jessica Powers entered Carmel of the Mother of God, a convent in her home state of Wisconsin. The following year, she took the name of Sister Miriam of the Holy Spirit. Far from the city that inspired this poem, we might imagine that she was still charged with those variations of light—how we may be washed by it, and yet also burned: a transfiguration.

* * *

"We need that dimension of sadness in our lives, don't we?" It was a statement of truth given the gentle lift of a question—a turn of syntax appropriate for a poet. Jessica Powers wrote those words in 1986, near the end of her life. She pondered how "the best literature and art has that undercurrent of sorrow." Although it was nearly a lifetime separated from her many years as a nun, Powers turned to her years in New York. There, in the bustling city, "I could hardly bear the beautiful music that drifted up to me from a lower apartment."[18] Although delivered in prose, it is a poetic rendering: a recognition that even though beautifully alive, the world must sometimes be stilled in order for the artist to create.

Born in Mauston, Wisconsin, in 1905, Powers was preternaturally formed by place. Her pastoral surroundings offered material and metaphor for poems steeped in spiritual longing, and it was in those settings where she experienced great emotional losses. Powers was baptized at St. Patrick's Church, and afterward attended a school in town where she was taught by Dominican sisters. Her attendance there was, in some ways, compulsory—her parish priest wanted children who hoped to receive their first Holy Communion to go to the school—although the circumstance resulted in a fortuitous coincidence for young Powers.[19]

She was mentored there by Sister Lucille Massart, a doting teacher who encouraged Powers to write poetry.[20] Like other younger writers,

Powers's early verse was about her family, but Massart remained in touch with her throughout high school, as her poetry became more ambitious. The sister gave books of poetry to Powers, including works by the Catholic poet Ruth Mary Fox, whose writing was steeped in Carmelite references and style.[21]

Powers went two hours southeast to Milwaukee, where she began studying at Marquette University, a Jesuit institution, in 1922. Her family, though, was unable to afford tuition, and she returned home the following year. A short stint in Chicago working as a typist for a manufacturing company was complicated by tuberculosis, but she read widely.[22] While in Chicago, she met a Dominican seminarian named Christopher Powell. They exchanged poems, ambitions, and emotional support; Powers called herself "a Simon of Cyrene to your cross,"[23] speaking to Powell's enduring depression. She had often confided in Powell her desire to move to the East Coast, and was pleased when the opportunity finally arose.

Despite the literary community afforded to her in New York City, Wisconsin remained on her mind. It was the only place, she would say, to which she "could apply both the adjectives rich and desolate."[24] In her poem "Escape," she writes: "I think: if I would lift this window now / and pause to listen, leaning on this sill, / I might hear, for my heart's full consolation / the whip-poor-wills on some Wisconsin hill."[25] That land compelled her back in mysterious ways. Wisconsin had shaped Powers's poetic vision, had made her a poet-mystic, and from her distant, urban vantage point, that mysticism called to her.

Powers attended a retreat led by a Jesuit and, likely fueled by the swells of devotion that follow guided prayer and reflection, she announced her desire to become a Carmelite nun. She would say that she needed strong structure in her life "lest I dream myself away."[26] The priest told her to pursue her vocation, although she soon discovered that all convents in Brooklyn and the Bronx were full. One new Carmelite monastery, though, was open to new sisters: in Milwaukee.[27] It seemed like a divine message, an opportunity for Powers the poet and Powers the mystic to become one.

The Carmelites lived an austere existence. They did not eat meat. They fasted from mid-September to Easter. They silently prayed for hours on end, speaking only during an hour of recreation in the morning and evening. Their bare-floored rooms had ivory-painted walls which were also bare save for Our Lady of Mount Carmel, and St. Teresa or St. John of the Cross. The only other objects in the room were a table, a chair, and straw-filled bed.[28]

Powers entered the monastery on June 24, 1941.[29] Although she had to leave later that year due to another bout of tuberculosis, she returned in the spring, and received the habit and veil of a novice in April 1942. She became Sister Miriam of the Holy Spirit, although she would always publish as Jessica Powers.[30] Her prioress, Mother Grace, supported her art; Powers's second book of poems, *The Place of Splendor*, was published the same year she professed her final vows. She would remain Sister Miriam for the rest of her life, serving several terms as prioress, battling the tuberculosis that plagued her from a younger age, managing the monastery's move from Milwaukee to Pewaukee, and continuing to write poetry.

* * *

In Powers we find a curious, provocative synthesis: a poet very much of an ambitious Catholic poetic renaissance, formed by a pastoral world but matured as a writer within an urban space—despite her longing for that former setting. Her poetry exists on the spectrum of work that is devotional and also jarring.

"I saw the world kissing its own darkness," she writes in "The Vision."[31] The poem's narrator wakes to see the sunrise, yet "suddenly over the hill a horde appeared / dragging a huge tarpaulin." The shadows cover "unwary land and hapless city," leaving "no sunrise," no dawn.

The narrator struggles through bushes and brambles in the forest and then reaches a dark city where people "moved to the loveless embrace of folly." An eerie bacchanal unfolds, as people danced to "music that was crazed with rhythm, / were themselves discord though they knew it not, / or if they knew, cared less."

The narrator ultimately finds a fire "burning, / shining and dancing" in a desert. She worries as the darkness surrounds it, but "The flame burned on, innocent, unimperiled. / There was no darkness that could put it out."[32]

The deeply symbolic poem contains themes that Powers revisited in "The Uninvited," first drafted in 1935 and revised in 1939 during her time in New York City. She writes of a city "that through time shall lie / in a fixed darkness of the earth and sky." The ones who walk those streets at night are "the lonely, the unloved, the weak and shy." These "outcast ones, the last, the least, / whom earth has not invited to her feast, / and who, were they invited in the end, / finding their wedding clothes too frayed to mend, / would not attend."[33]

While Powers certainly wrote devotional verse that followed the expectations of the genre, poems like these exist as curiosities: they reside within their dark journeys, rather than build toward a simple religious conclusion. She often invokes landscape imagery; the sense of her narrators either literally or metaphorically looking across a distance, a movement of the sky and light.

When her narrators do arrive at belief, the results are often ecstatic. In "Young Maidens Running," a poem invoked to novices, she initially defines a saint as "a slow serene / candle in a cathedral solitude, / a virgin lily in a nameless wood." Yet in the final stanza of the poem, she opts for a more charged belief: "Hence must I now for saint a new concept tell: / a maiden racing toward a sole desire / with garments glowing and her face on fire."[34]

Her paean to "Abraham" is a wonderful, skilled sketch of an oft-written character: "I love Abraham, that old weather-beaten / unwavering nomad; when God called to him, / no tender hand wedged time into his stay." Stirred by God, Abraham was "erupted" into his long trek, imbued with a divine confidence: "How could he think his ancient thigh would bear / nations, or how consent that Isaac die, / with never an outcry nor an anguished prayer?"[35]

Rather than reside solely in archetype, though, the poem turns toward the contemporary narrator. She thinks "how I manipulate

/ dates and decisions, pull apart the dark, / dally with doubts here and with counsel there, / take out old maps and stare." Worried that, compared to her sage predecessor, her faith may be slight, she invokes him: "Was there a call at all, my fears remark. / I cry out: Abraham, old nomad you, / are you my father? Come to me in pity. / Mine is a far and lonely journey, too."[36]

Even that lonely journey is a gift, as she writes in another poem: "If you have nothing, gather back your sigh / and with your hands held high, your heart held high, / lift up your emptiness."[37]

Her poem "But Not With Wine" begins with an epigraph from Isaiah 51:21, "You are drunk, but not with wine." The narrator is taken, almost enraptured, with belief. She concludes in the second stanza: "If there be indecorum in my songs, / fasten the blame where rightly it belongs: / on Him who offered me too many cups / of His most potent goodness—not on me, / a peasant who, because a king was host, / drank out of courtesy."

Another poem, "Counsel for Silence," also arises from Scripture: God's call for Elijah to rest in the Kerith Ravine, where he will be fed by ravens. Powers adopts a divine second-person for the single-stanza sonnet. The recipient is counseled to leave "without ceremony of departure" so that the air may "speak the mystery of your absence." Powers's narrator seeks to reveal how the mind, through prayer and faith, can reach an emotional distance without a literal journey. She notes how others, "Seeing the body present, they will wonder / Where went the secret soul." In order for true prayerful journey to occur, the penitent must be a "pilgrim with no ties to earth." Instead, she must "Walk out alone and make the never told / Your healing distance and your anchorhold / And let the ravens feed you. [38]

Her sense of divine love is captured concisely in lines from another poem: "I would define my love in some incredible penance / of which no impotent language is aware."[39] In a letter written on Ash Wednesday in 1987, Powers wrote that she came to seek the "contradictions and crosses of life" with "a certain joy—signs that tell me that Jesus is near."[40] Her list of maledictions are mundane: the "unexpected delay, the negative response, the inopportune caller, the gimmick that won't work, the nice food that got overcooked, the lack of something needed, the ballpoint pen that smudges, the mistake one can't undo."[41] Powers thinks these frustrations "are so much richer than the penances I pick out for myself."[42]

Poetry, in some way, was a vehicle for both appreciation and penance. No matter her mode of emotion, her ultimate subject was the natural world, and how that world reflected in her soul. "Earth keeps its seasons and its liturgy," she writes, "as should the soul. Oh, come, green summer, blur / these wastes and let my soul in song declare / Who came by flesh and Who by fire to her."[43] Creation of God transcended the "impotent language" of humans. "My heart believes," she wrote in her poem "In This Green Wood," "though dawn and evening / are wholly hallowed, / none match a midday / with lighted leaves."[44] After all, as she writes elsewhere, "Behold, all places which have light in them / truly are Bethlehem."[45]

Although such light and beauty are fragile and tenuous, those precarities are part of their divinity. "Now that the bright red berries lend / color to the June berry tree," she writes in "Richer Berry," "my need is urgent to befriend / denial and austerity."[46] She writes of this gentle temptation in supple language: "I touch the fruit with lips of wish / and with the fingers of soft words, / and leave them, a delicious dish / in taste and substance, to the birds." She arrives at a later understanding: "No husk, no shell after the rich / full fruit shall dull my later day. / I shall take hunger first, on which / the spirit thrives best, anyway."[47]

Powers strikes a refreshingly honest, and yet simultaneously affirming tone in her poems: the world is full of beautiful enticements (some of them outright temptations), and yet the spirit is not filled with those prosaic treats. It is enough that the beauty of this world is a pleasant ornamentation for the journey, and the natural world of her childhood Wisconsin is the perfect fodder for these contemplations. While the stirring grandeur and transformative shadows of the city compelled Powers to write in figurative modes, her writing about pastoral Wisconsin is contrastingly tactile.

In "Return," she laments that ambition is never enough for our souls: "This was the fever that beset my years, / that led by pride, I put my aim too high. / I strained my spirit, grasping at the moon; / my heart I wearied, reaching for the sky."[48] It was not enough. The narrator realizes that she "must come home again to simple things: / robins and buttercups and bumblebees, / laugh with the elves and try again to find / a leprechaun behind the hawthorn trees."[49]

Likewise, in the aptly titled "The Valley of My Childhood," the narrator writes of a creek filled with minnows, and a forested shore full of "wary killdeer and wading crane." A field of wild strawberries and thick moss. Marshes, full of frogs and cattails, formed the borders of their play areas. Owl and raccoon out under the moon. Although separated from that tranquil space for years, once back, "the long complaining / dies in my throat."[50]

Powers's pastoral vision is appreciative but not unrealistic. In fact, the beautiful world is not only beyond our comprehension of language—a recognition that places her in the literary and theological lineage of Gerard Manley Hopkins—it is a world that transcends our understanding. As a creation of the divine, it is for us to appreciate but not fully catalog. In "The Cedar Tree," she describes how cedar branches bend low "under the full exhaustion of the snow." As a poet and sister, Powers wants to remind us that what happens next is of grand design: "And since He set no wind of day to rising, / this burden of beauty and this burden of cold, / (whether the wood breaks or the branches hold) / must be of His devising."[51]

Beauty, in the end, was Powers's great song. "The desirable thing about beauty," she once wrote, "is that we can find great rapture in it, without any consideration of our own inadequacies." When she thought of the love of God, she "became aware of my own emptiness of heart; when I think of the goodness of God, I recall my innumerable needs; when I think of the mercy of God, I remember my own failures." Yet when she thinks of the beauty of God—and we might say, when she breathes that beauty through poetry—"I cease to exist at all, I become a living adoration."[52]

Through poetry, and her cloistered life, Powers embraced a God-shaped beauty. As first a longtime homemaker and later a member of a burgeoning literary community, she experienced the domestic and secular world, before turning to an ascetic existence shaped by her pastoral mysticism. She considers her Carmelite existence in "Enclosure," a poem written within her first decade as a nun. Calling herself a "Gypsy by nature," she wonders how she might "endure" the "small strict space" of the convent with its "meager patch of sky?" The first half of the poem is largely marked by a series of questions; an anxious narrator worried that she has made a mistake. She fears that "madness" has "possessed" her to come to this place, fearing that she might "deed it to myself until I die."

She even intones Teresa of Ávila, the sixteenth-century Carmelite mystic, unsure how the visionary might "approve" of a life characterized by "wailing, barring, minimizing, shrinking." Yet the narrator, and likely Powers, discovers the walled constraints are edifying because they force the action of imagination. In mind, heart, and poem, she found a way to travel without end: "Its trails outrun the most adept explorer, / outweigh the gypsy's most inordinate need. / Its heights cry out to mystic and adorer. / Oh, here are space and distances indeed."[53] Although Powers worried that "when self intrudes on the art, prayer is lost," her collected poetry is a mystic's search for divine beauty: a search that brought her from Wisconsin to New York City, and then back home, to an enclosure that sustained rather than stifled a rangy mind.[54]

2

SISTER MARY BERNETTA QUINN: WOMAN OF LETTERS

"INDULGENT, OR CANDID, or uncommon reader / —I've some: a wife, a nun, a ghost or two—" wrote Randall Jarrell, the critic and poet.[1] The line was not fiction. Jarrell had a regular reader, who was also a sharp critic, and a witty correspondent. In April 1948, the poet Wallace Stevens received a letter from the same sister. Her name was Sister Mary Bernetta Quinn (1915–2003), and she was completing her PhD at the University of Wisconsin. It was their first correspondence, and she'd enclosed some notes on his poetry, for which Stevens was thankful: "It is a relief to have a letter from someone that is interested in understanding."[2]

A few years later, adding to his burgeoning acclaim, Stevens won the Pulitzer Prize for his *Collected Poems*. Even praiseworthy reviews, though, often misread his poetic intentions. Stevens knew the gift of having a sensitive, adept reader, and Quinn was just the right audience.

Despite having never met, Stevens felt comfortable sharing his poetic and personal visions with Quinn; he wrote his first response to her a day or two after receiving her initial letter. However brief, his note to her includes a curious personal admission: "I do seek a centre and expect to go on seeking it."[3] The spiritual gesture appeared more than incidental.

Their letters continued, for Stevens found in Quinn an erudite and spiritual correspondent. Each letter from her, he wrote, was "a flash apart from the endless common-place."[4] In 1951, after a literary critic detected a sense of spiritual "nothingness" in his poetry, Stevens wrote Quinn with a clarification: "I am not an atheist although I do not believe to-day in the same God in whom I believed when I was a boy."[5] Considering the debate over Stevens's deathbed conversion to Catholicism, his heartfelt letters to Quinn are tantalizing. What made a mystically inclined, complex poet comfortable sending such honest thoughts from Hartford, Connecticut, to Winona, Minnesota?

* * *

While walking the campus of the College of St. Teresa in Winona, Minnesota, Roselyn Viola Quinn was struck by the sight of the Chapel of St. Mary of the Angels, known as the heart of the college. Completed less than a decade before she enrolled at the school, the grand chapel stirred many a heart, and Quinn appreciated the description by a fellow student of the chapel at twilight: "before the lights are lit, but while the campanile cross above sends forth its shining beams. No one else is there just now, but a strangely singing heart tells you that Someone is there. The gleaming cross without, to light the way; the gentle Presence within, to welcome you—Beauty visible and invisible."[6]

Young Quinn felt that presence, and entered the Franciscan Sister of the Congregation of Our Lady of Lourdes in 1934, taking the name Mary Bernetta. Born September 19, 1915, in Lake Geneva, Wisconsin, nearly four hours to the southeast of campus, Quinn had been drawn to the small women's school, whose original description of students was both apt and inspiring for her curious mind: "She should have the broadest, the deepest, the highest culture of heart and mind."[7]

Several years after professing her vows, Quinn received a BA from the college, where she would later teach for over a decade and serve as department chair. She received her doctorate in English in 1952 from the University of Wisconsin-Madison for a dissertation titled "Metamorphosis in Modern American Poetry" that was soon excerpted in an issue of *The Sewanee Review*.

Quinn's identity as a writer was inextricable from her dynamic work as a teacher. In addition to teaching at St. Teresa, Quinn would go on to teach at several historically Black universities, including Allen University and Norfolk State University. She taught abroad for a year at Meiji Gakuin University and the University of the Sacred Heart in Tokyo, and later at the International Yeats Summer School in Sligo. Her visiting professorships included Siena College, SUNY-Buffalo, and the Catholic University of America. She received grants in nonfiction writing and biography from the National Endowment for the Arts and the National Endowment for the Humanities, and completed residencies at Yaddo and the MacDowell Colony.[8]

A revised version of her dissertation was published in 1955 as *The Metamorphic Tradition in Modern Poetry*, including chapters on Stevens, Ezra Pound, William Carlos Williams, T. S. Eliot, Hart Crane, Randall Jarrell, and W. B. Yeats. Allen Tate, the influential poet, critic, editor, and recent convert to Catholicism, read portions of her book in manuscript. In her introduction to the book, Quinn describes metamorphosis as capturing "man's desire and need to transcend the psychologically repressive conditions of his mechanized *milieu*."[9]

Quinn's formative milieu was the Catholic classroom. Students remembered her as humble, despite her literary pedigree. Her classes were steeped in poetry: both the writing of verse and the analysis of published work. She asked her students to fold submitted work "in half lengthwise," perhaps an action both practical and symbolic to lessen the grading load.[10]

One of Quinn's students, Marilynn Hallen, told me that one of their assignments "was to compare a poem of either Ezra Pound or Wallace Stevens to one of Peter Hurd's artworks," an ekphrastic exercise that revealed how poetry "lived in every form of artwork." Hallen felt as if Quinn "seemed to understand each [poet's] deepest thoughts," although she never mentioned her correspondence with famous poets.

Her correspondence was extensive. Quinn's letters create a web in which she is at the center of personal, spiritual, and literary conversations with many of the finest poets of her generation, all of whom found her to be an especially witty interlocutor. It is not unheard of for poets and writers to receive missives from those in religious life; such a spiritual existence is preternaturally focused on texts as living, generative objects. Yet Quinn's correspondents saw her not merely as novel, but essential.

In addition to her correspondence with Stevens, Quinn exchanged letters with Denise Levertov, William Carlos Williams, Robert Penn Warren, James Wright, Seamus Heaney, and others. She read their work with skilled attention, and they responded to her with sincerity and gratitude.

Wright, in many ways, thought of Quinn as his confessor. "It is just about daybreak," Wright intones in a 1964 letter. "After an entire night of work, and a dawning moment, I suddenly turned to write you a few words, in obedience to an impulse no, it is a voice, not an 'impulse' from within. The voice speaks very often, and it occurs to me just now that perhaps I need only try to follow the voice out of the many voices, the one that bids me stand and live."[11] Perennially wracked by depression, Wright found "a beautiful solace, a real joy, in speaking to you this way—answering you, almost."[12] Their correspondence would last for a decade. Wright affirmed that he was buoyed from a "bleak despair" by her words.[13]

"You must remember years ago how I told you of my love for you; and you certainly remain one of the persons most beloved to me in all my life," he wrote in 1974.[14] Wright told Quinn that whenever he heard of her or her writings—a frequent occurrence, due to her regular publication in prestigious literary magazines—he thought of their friendship. Yet his heart seemed also to be stirred by some form of spiritual love. Wright assured Quinn that he thought of her when he was "in the presence of some grandeur, as in Italy or in the mountains of New York, or even when I am feeling sad about something—the last because I know that you would understand the sadness, even if no one else on earth did."[15]

Quinn even inspired Wright to read *The Cloud of Unknowing*, a fourteenth-century mystical work that seemed written for a soul such as his. The unnamed author assures his reader that the desire to seek God will be slowed by a darkness, a cloud of unknowing; a frustrating distance from the divine. "And so prepare to remain in this darkness as long as you can," Wright would read, the expanse of the mountains in front of him, "always begging for him you love; for if you are ever to feel or see him, so far as is possible in this life, it must always be in this cloud and this darkness."[16]

* * *

In September 1948, Stevens again wrote Quinn with a note of appreciation, saying "I cannot tell you how happy it made me to think that my poems have given any pleasure to a woman of your intelligence and goodwill."[17] In 1949, she sent him an Easter card that included a reference to the lion of Judah (a symbolic figure for Christ from the Book of Revelation), a detail which he then included in his poem "An Ordinary Evening in New Haven."

She continued to send Stevens letters at Easter and Christmas. His December response in 1951 is lyric. Hartford was "covered with snow and ice...But we have been having the most saintly moonlight nights."[18] Tired of the "roaring" of the Christmas season, he envied the "loneliness" of Quinn's empty college campus, where "one can collect one's self and no doubt, in your case, collect a great deal more."[19] In other letters, he expressed gratitude that Quinn's "notes bring me into contact with something that I should not have otherwise except for them."[20] Her letters "seem to come from something fundamental, something isolated from this ruthless present."[21]

Some critics use Stevens's conversion as the flashlight to uncover the religious themes in his poetry. Such an approach can be taken too far, but Stevens did regularly thank Quinn for the attention she paid to the "smaller things" in his verse, which often included religious allusions and concepts.[22] She never thought him a devotional poet; he never even thought himself a philosophical one (in May 1952, he told her: "If I felt the obligation to pursue the philosophy of my poems, I should be writing philosophy, not poetry; and it is poetry that I want to write").[23]

Quinn's keen critical eye also earned the praise of William Carlos Williams, who called her reading of *Paterson* "something of second sight." Williams thought Quinn unique: "Certainly it frightens me to see, rather than how obscure it is to others' minds, how clear it is to you. It shows me that since someone has looked discerningly into its motivations then others *may* see as much."[24]

In that letter from August 1951, Williams jokes that "You realize, of course, being a Catholic, that I am not a Catholic." Yet he thinks it a "great virtue" of Quinn that she did not "lay imputations" against his agnosticism: "You and I share something bigger than ourselves when we are tolerant—each of the other—as I have seen you to be."[25]

He again praised her religious sense upon the publication of her first book, *The Metamorphic Tradition in Modern Poetry* (1955), noting that a generosity of spirit illuminated her critical work: "You reveal yourself to be a religious person by something not easy to isolate and of which you never speak; that, to me, is the book's outstanding characteristic and one which gives it its unique distinction."[26]

Quinn's critical methods are a template for critics of faith, who wish to use their religious worldview as a source of metaphor and perception, rather than an ideological hammer. In her discussion of Robert Frost's poem "Nothing Gold Can Stay," in the shadow of his reading at John F. Kennedy's inauguration, Quinn ends a thematic explication for high school teachers with spiritual flourish: "Without committing Frost to any theology, some may interpret its relevance to life as a variation of an old proverb: 'God gives, and God takes away.' If God takes away, He gives something else in recompense: for spring, summer; for innocence, experience; for sunrise, full moon."[27]

Without directly interrogating Wallace Stevens's religious pondering, Quinn observes a curious analogy in his poem "Peter Quince at the Clavier": "Beauty is momentary in the mind, / But in the flesh it is immortal." She considers the Latin *incarnari*, "to be made flesh," and which can also mean "the giving of actual form to or making real"—a metamorphic rendering that corresponds to Stevens's idea in the poem that "poetry, painting, or music" can render beauty "permanent."[28]

Elsewhere, Quinn cast literary archetypes as foundationally, or experientially, religious. She opined that the "theme of the greatest literature, from THE ILIAD on, has always been purification through suffering, since after all this is the secret—an open one for those who look—of human existence itself."[29]

She had also begun to publish her own poetry. *Dancing in Stillness* (1983), her only book, collects work from those years. Flannery O'Connor had praised Quinn's verse, telling a Jesuit priest about "the Sister at Minneapolis that writes such good poetry."[30] A critic's sensitive analysis rarely translates to artistic skill, yet Quinn's letter relationships with poets suggest a true emotional investment in life and story. In her criticism and her correspondence, Quinn regularly engaged with the finest writers of her generation; however little known, her poems are unsurprisingly gentle and attentive.

"You have brought me here to show me a secret thing," she begins her poem "In Branches of Spruce." The narrator sits on a garden bench, and is thinking how no one else but her can see "a trembling square / of cobweb" in the spruce tree. Although the gift is temporary—"this cloth of silver and pearl the sun will sever, / this veil of Veronica the wind will tear"—it feels like a divine gift: "You have given me this cobweb strung with rain / like a father's whispered word to silence pain."[31]

Quinn lived in a space where faith and melancholy reside, but she was more interested in conversation and consolation than conversion. After James Wright gave a reading at the College of St. Teresa, she sent him comforting words: "When you first walked down the platform I was struck by what I recognized later was sadness…[don't let] gentle seriousness…sink into solemnity, lest the ghost of Theodore Roethke haunt you."[32]

She knew those solemn places well—at least in her poetry. She begins "Bernard" with a plain-spoken darkness: "Do you remember, brother, that night / When we as children walked home from the movie / Wondering as we crossed the park / Who would die first, Mother or Dad?" The narrator recalls how her brother was grief-stricken at their mother's death, but when "Dad died, you didn't come at all." She pauses for a question, and answer—in the final stanza: "Why do I ask you now if you remember? / You are out of earshot, with the rest of the dead."[33]

Quinn often pivots from the sentimental to the sublime. Early in "Childhood," she writes of youth: "Let us go back again to the tiger lilies, / The front porch swing squeaking in the summer night." Her clever phrases alight what could become cliche: "The afternoons on the grass under the leaves of June / While the radio talked on the other side of the wall; / The child's fingers picking the bright nasturtiums, / Or dusting the endless rungs of the aunt's stair." Yet her final stanza upends the dream: "Did they exist, or did I dream they happened? / Give me the key to enter the real world / Where everything is always what it seems."[34]

Her tendency to include questions serves multiple functions. Quinn is conversational without becoming laconic. In "Mirror for Ghosts," she writes of a night full of "invisible things," unspoken words that "flutter through the silence in nervous rings, / Making a sound of leaf-fall, or Carmelites praying." She then begins a sequence of second-person-focused questions: inquiries for the reader, or perhaps herself, as to whether one might recognize the mysteries among us: "If the unborn took shape in air like raindrops, though clearer, / Friend, would you bid them welcome with a smile, / Holding a future love up to them like a mirror?"

Whether she ends with a certain darkness, or a question without an answer, Quinn was comfortable with a lack of reconciliation within her poems. One short poem meditates on the prophet Isaiah, leading with an epigraph from 38:13: "You have folded up my life like a weaver who severs the last thread." "It is over," she begins, "The scenes where /

The nights when / The hands that / The fears which / And I lie in your hands, / A cloth that the weaver has finished."[35] The epigrammatic style, largely devoid of punctuation, feels in the tradition of William Carlos Williams, yet renders a distinctly biblical vision.

Although Quinn did not often write of her own life as a sister, one notable exception is "A Sister Meditates." A sister begins an "hour to pray for peace, herself the channel." She moves her "lawn chair out of the sun, / Counts misty mushrooms in the sky's wide garden." Sounds of John Coltrane "shimmer" from a nearby open window. Despite her earnest devotion, from the "heat, clovery grass, sweet william" and "brushing of a low-hung cherry branch / Against her hair," she falls asleep.[36]

Her dream is a panoply of metaphor and arresting image, a marked contrast to the calm Evanston afternoon in which she naps. First, the sister imagines a desert scene where drops of blood fall from the sky and "dry to clots smaller than nailheads." The hour of Christ's crucifixion arrives, punctuated by a storm that lights the sky. Then the poem fragments into a surreal depiction of Christ, his "heart, nuclear-strong, / Wakes in the body wound about with linens, / Now forever burned by radiation."[37]

The sister awakens and feels "His gaze upon her." She thinks of the final line of the Franciscan prayer—"It is in dying we are born"— and the poem ends with a characteristically jarring line for Quinn: "Calmly / She rises to die."[38]

Here Quinn's critical aesthetic illuminates her own work. No matter whether she was writing of W. B. Yeats, Wallace Stevens, T. S. Eliot, or even prose writers like J. F. Powers, Quinn was most interested in the mode of metamorphosis. Quinn was a generous critic. Her *ars poetica* for her critical sense is instructive: "One of the chief services which criticism can render—a service of more value than awarding praise or condemning—is to construct with humility and a perseverance brightened with sympathy some map drawn from a position in the upper air of objectivity and designed to reduce the effort required for appreciation—a short cut, if you will, to the reader's rightful joy in the full aesthetic realization of the poem."[39]

Quinn imagined the role of the critic as not judge but guide. For her, the metamorphic tradition was essential to understanding the work of her contemporaries, and since metamorphosis is both essential and transformational, her belief in the transfiguring power of Christ anchored her critical acumen while enabling her to engage with largely secular work. She noted that metamorphosis "is but another term to express Saint Paul's admonition that man should put on the new man, Christ."[40]

Metamorphosis, Quinn argued, was "one resolution of the question of transience," an Ovidian recognition of the "cyclic character of the universe."[41] Williams and Stevens were her great lodestars in that vision. She considered Williams to be Joycean, one "magnetized by dream imagery" who, like "the Surrealist painters," channeled "weird fantasies" of imagination as they mined "the unconscious in their hunt for inspiration."[42]

Quinn was fond of Williams's attraction to dreams and sleep, noting that the poet once gave a speech about how the "first signs" of imagination's "approach" are "like those of falling asleep," a Yeatsian conception of transformation of self into artist.[43] In that transformative state, distortion was inevitable—yet poets and artists "distort in order to make visible what the waking eye is blind to."[44] Quinn thought that Williams shared that gift with Stevens. She quoted lines from his poem "Bouquet of Roses in Sunlight" to illustrate how "no one sees quite the same rose as anyone else does": sense "is like a flow of meanings with no speech / And of as many meanings as of men."[45]

A sister, a teacher, a critic, a correspondent, and a reader, Quinn was a literary node, so her foundational vision of metamorphosis as endemic to the poetic art and worldview is appropriate. To note that one of the most flexible and perceptive readers of a generation is a nun is not being provincial; Quinn was a scholar of literary culture and a participant within it, and such duality both arose from and was revealed through her idea of metamorphosis.

Quinn envisioned metamorphosis as connecting "the realm of reality with the realm of the imagination," clarifying that those spheres of perception were in fact the same, "a complex and ever-flowing system of resemblances."[46] Of all art forms, poetry was replete with the metamorphic urge. When our imagination observes similarities and connections, that imagination "intensifies reality, enhances it, heightens it," a poetic theory in the tradition of Gerard Manley Hopkins's radical vision of inscape.[47]

In fact, Quinn's critical observations of her contemporaries might be applied to her own work: "The poet will not submit, then, to that chrysalis which rationalists keep telling him is his true domain. Consciously and subconsciously, he wants to transcend the limits of his senses, the boundaries of matter. As a consequence, he struggles; and his struggle, with its outcome, is recorded in that current which is metamorphosis in modern poetry."[48]

Quinn believed that "to write a poem is in itself to effect a metamorphosis," and her poems accomplish those encounters between the divine and mundane.[49] In "Mary," Quinn writes to the Blessed Mother that she imagines her "in the gold canoe of the moon" or "sometimes on earth, where I can see your eyes."[50] For Quinn, as a poet, God must always be thought of through our faculties and experiences. While in the past, poets "could write without apology and directly upon such abstractions as melancholy, the vanity of human wishes, imagination," contemporary sensibility "requires that these be translated into the concrete, and the personages of myth and folklore stand ready in the poet's mind to accomplish the translation."[51]

Myth perfected could be found in Christ, about whom Quinn reflects in "Holy Saturday at Claremont Manor," a poem that weds past with present in the eternity of Christian belief. "I am alone here on this bench," she says, "Within me plains of salt-white sand." She is far from birds, wind, or even darkness, which might "offer me the shelter of a friend." Yet she finds solace that life continues, for, in the shadow of Easter, "somewhere in Asia Minor / In a grave where no other corpse has lain / A heart is beginning to beat."[52]

Quinn died in 2003, leaving unfinished the draft of a prose version of Dante's *Divine Comedy* for children, titled *Pilgrimage to the Stars*. A surprising adaptation, but Sister Bernetta seemed to have particular gifts of transformation, literary or otherwise. In one of his final letters to her, Stevens wrote of how there was a calming rhythm to her seasonal notes to him. Those epistles "Somehow or other, take me back to a much simpler world of home which, while it is gone for good, is still a good deal more permanent than the present world can ever be."[53] As a Catholic, Quinn did not fear death; perhaps its presence in her life allowed her to render such varying emotional modes in her poem. When the poet Randall Jarrell died, she eulogized their friendship in a poem that ends with a heartfelt line: "And death is no fence, but a bridge to where you are."[54]

It is one thing—and not a little thing—for a mid-century sister devoted to teaching and service to regularly publish poetry and criticism in the most prestigious publications of her time. It is fascinating, though, for that same woman to be at the center of a dizzying web of letters; to be the pivot or axis of artistic and personal conversation for so many poets. She was a close friend to many, and her unique sense made her feel like the best literary friend they could hope for: a humble, invested soul.

The word *critic* often implies one who casts blithe aspersions: one who is perpetually unsatisfied and unmoved. Quinn offers another, more dynamic model. Her manner and mode of criticism was itself a type of poetics, in which the critic has a utilitarian and aesthetic function. Her extended analyses of modern poets were a mixture of close-reading and spiritually informed contemplation; it is no wonder that stylists as varied as Stevens and Williams found her attention to be a gift.

Her *ars poetica* of criticism was based on Saint Augustine's suggestion: "Love so that you may understand."[55] Quinn wished to inhabit the work of those she examined: not from a distance, nor from a perch, but from within. Through the work of writers she admired, she "assume[d] the role of preceptor, a word stemming from *praecipire*, 'to know beforehand,'" so that she could "[promulgate] working rules respecting the techniques of an art."[56] She thought the highest level of criticism "aims at making some contribution toward a *paideuma*, or culture, by the discovery of relationships among certain literary phenomena, leading to a body of knowledge necessary for the substructure of a cultured society."[57]

Quinn deftly fit that role. Inspired by Ezra Pound's "A Few Don'ts by an Imagiste," Quinn created "A Few Do's for Critics." "Weed out famous but inconsequential writing," she advised, "in order to concentrate on the classics." Read widely, and "compare." Turn the critical eye inward, "in line with the meaning of *criticize*": "to pick out for oneself." It was essential that every critic "learn to distinguish between 'inventors' and 'masters.'" Finally, understand a genre by reading back to its genesis.[58] These suggestions were meant to cultivate the critical acumen of those whose careful reading and writing might contribute to the broader culture: to form a sensibility of art that might transform perception. She hoped for nothing less than a metamorphosis.

In "The Terrible Tower Unlocked," a 1959 essay, Quinn considers the challenges of communication, in life and literature. "The modern American writer feels these limitations which the body imposes, but he is not resigned," she affirms. Communication has two modes which affect the artist and critic. First, "there is the very structure of his work itself, made out of symbols which must also serve for our use as daily verbal expression of thought, a use which tends to enervate it for his needs." Next, the necessary and "explicit recognition of the failure of language," coupled with the ardent desire for a "refreshing of language so that human beings may once more share a spiritual as well as a physical world."[59]

That tension is a ripe space for a capable critic. Sister Mary Bernetta Quinn is best understood in the tradition of Hilda, and yet evolving that lineage; a woman religious who patronized her contemporaries through her skilled criticism and her kenotic correspondence, but who joined them as a skilled artist.

3

MADELINE DEFREES: THE SPRINGS OF SILENCE

IN LATE 1961 and early 1962, a trio of esteemed American poets—Robert Lowell, Stanley Kunitz, and Louise Bogan—judged the Helen Burlin Memorial Award for the 92nd Street Young Men's and Young Women's Hebrew Association. "Terrible stuff, mostly," Bogan lamented, as she trudged through the batches of book manuscripts delivered by the Poetry Center's ballet-studying secretary. Bogan's only saving grace: "I'll get paid for this."[1]

The prestigious first book award, which carried a $1,500 prize, and started the publishing career of Ted Hughes, future British Poet Laureate, had over 200 submissions. Lowell favored the manuscript of Frederick Seidel, whom Bogan thought was a "big, wild, hallucinatory manic."[2] Although Lowell managed to push through his selection when the judges conferred, they awarded an honorable mention to "a little nun from Spokane" named Sister Mary Gilbert. She had been encouraged to submit her manuscript to the competition by the poet and anthologist Samuel Hazo, who had a particular interest in poetry with spiritual concerns.[3] Bogan, in particular, was drawn to Gilbert: "She sees things rather panoramically, and is not at all pietistic—hardly any Jesus and NO Holy Mother. Unusual."[4] It was an observation both prescient and prophetic.

* * *

Two years later, Sister Mary Gilbert of the Sisters of the Holy Names of Jesus and Mary, born Madeline DeFrees (1919–2015), published her book manuscript. *From the Darkroom* (1964) was lauded in *the New*

York Times: "her lines deliver the laconic music that reassembles reality in a smiting chord."[5] DeFrees also received acclaim for her fiction, including a story, "The Model Chapel," that appeared in the *Virginia Quarterly Review* and was selected for *The Best American Short Stories* of 1962, alongside work by Arthur Miller, John Updike, and Flannery O'Connor.

DeFrees's story perfectly encapsulates the minutiae of religious life. A nun, Sister Constance, is asked to "write a little poem" to put on plastic piggy banks, strategically placed throughout the convent house during a fundraiser.[6] She escapes the job, but "cringed at the sight" of the hokey typewritten messages taped to the banks: "A fervent prayer / An extra penny / For our new chapel / To sanctify many."[7]

When Sister Constance enters the chapel, and sees a "dressed-up doll with a crown of gilt and pearls," she says a "prayer of atonement and not of petition." As a young nun, "she might have felt obliged to muffle her distaste for cheap religious art. Now she knew that God does not demand suspension of the critical faculties; that obedience and intelligence, taste even, can be reconciled without compromise."[8]

DeFrees's story dramatizes the worry that devotional writing can become trite; a sentiment she voiced following media attention to the release of *From the Darkroom*. The book's front cover features a centered white cross; on the back jacket, a photo of DeFrees in habit, hands crossed over an open book. "I think nuns might be more reluctant than laymen to write religious poetry," DeFrees said in a newspaper profile a year after the book was released. "I find, for instance, that many of the symbols that are meaningful to me don't communicate to other people. Also, if you are using this material you have to be very good or you will really fall flat."[9]

DeFrees's life was steeped in literature. Her poetry appeared widely; poems in her debut had been previously published in *America, Beloit Poetry Journal, Minnesota Review, New York Times, Northwest Review, Poetry Northwest, Prairie Schooner, Sewanee Review,* and *Spirit.* An associate professor at Holy Names College in Spokane, WA, she worked as a visiting professor at Seattle University, a Jesuit college, after the book was released. She received her BA in English from Marylhurst College in 1948, and her MA in journalism from the University of Oregon in 1951, her first secular education.

DeFrees was born in 1919, in Ontario, Oregon, and attended St. Matthew's grade school where she was taught by the Sisters of Saint Mary of Beaverton, Oregon. "Most of them were girls straight off the farm, and not very well educated. I loved my first grade teacher, but in general they used to send us the older, crabby nuns, because we had boys who were hard to manage."[10] Her family wanted her to continue a Catholic education, but in a more intellectual environment, so she moved in with her uncle in Portland so that she could attend St. Mary's Academy.

DeFrees was immediately drawn to the Sisters of the Holy Names, who taught at the school: nuns "who found time for tennis and basketball between classes and prayers, and who seemed to be so thoroughly in touch with the modern girl at the same time that they had just enough reserve to command my respect and pique my curiosity."[11] They also had a sense of humor: "One of the nuns who knew me best in those [high school] days says that I made her think of a Packard motor in a Ford chassis."[12] After graduating high school, she entered the order on July 27, 1936, at sixteen years old.[13]

Her decision was a mixture of practicality and piety. "There wasn't much for a woman to do at that time," she reflected, and the worldly nuns had made an impression on her.[14] Her call to religious life "was not a miraculous voice or a luminous vision from heaven," but rather "the desire to serve God in a special way," despite "a certain natural repugnance to make the sacrifices involved."[15] DeFrees documented her entry into the novitiate within *The Springs of Silence*, her first book of prose, published in 1953. The opening scene captures her wit. Teenage DeFrees muses about the convent's meticulous rules: "pen and pencil sets had to be trimmed in silver and not in gold. Office book and missal must have red, rather than gilt, edges."[16] All of her clothes and accessories must be black, including leather suitcase, silk gloves, stockings. She wonders: "How do nuns go into mourning?"[17]

The Springs of Silence is a valuable document of American mid-century religious life, steeped in refreshingly honest anecdotes. While in high school, DeFrees would come home and kneel before a statue of the Blessed Mother. She said three Hail Marys each evening in hopes that she might one day become a nun. "Sometimes," she reminisces, "I felt that the petition was a little short of hypocrisy. I'd come in after a dance or a show, glowing with the excitement of the evening, and kneel for the routine invocation. It seemed to me that I hardly meant the prayer at all; but, deep down, the determination was still there, even if temporarily obscured by the glitter of colored lights."[18]

DeFrees was drawn to the atmospheric qualities of the convent. The halls were "places of silence," a rule that had both practical and spiritual origins.[19] Silence during movement afforded nuns an opportunity for contemplation: a walking prayer of preparation. Prayer, in fact, was best done frequently, "not something formal and perfunctory, to be pursued only in the chapel." Prayer "was a spirit pervading the entire day and every action of it."[20] Although DeFrees admitted being drawn to "the self-sacrifice, the simplicity, and the generosity embodied in the religious vocation," her writing avoids reductive depictions of convent life, and remains aware of stereotypes.[21] Those who view nuns as "staid" see "exterior likenesses only—the dignified deportment, the quiet composure. They assume that these traits are inborn and not cultivated. As a result, they identify natural reticence and innate severity with a call to religious life."[22]

Being a sister was an *active* form of presentation and persona; a cultivation, DeFrees writes, anchored in recursive prayer. Although the religious rule severely "regulates exterior conduct," internal traits are almost refracted: sisters hold "intense differences" within themselves, and between each other.[23] Although obedience to God's will was spiritually good, it required attention and action. Late in the book, DeFrees makes an observation that feels directed at misperceptions of sisters: "Sometimes I wonder whether anyone outside the convent can really know a nun. Even those who are closest to her—members of her immediate family—can't completely bridge the gulf between the world and the cloister."[24] These sisters were decidedly human.

"In the novitiate, everyone wrote poetry," DeFrees later recalled. "There's a natural high that comes from versifying, and people were always writing letters home and putting verses in."[25] One of her superiors, in fact, "told me that I wasn't anything special just because I was a poet," a comment that makes "The Model Chapel" appear steeped in actual experience.[26] Another mentor praised DeFrees's writing, but told the young nun to stick to prose. "Most women don't have the freedom to be really great poets," she warned.[27] After DeFrees received the finalist nod for her *From the Darkroom* manuscript, she studied on scholarship with the Catholic poet John Berryman at the School of Letters at Indiana University, Bloomington. DeFrees stood out, "swathed in five yards of black wool serge."[28] "He picked on me mercilessly," DeFrees said. "He liked to pose as the authority on all things Catholic, and so it didn't matter what I said, he would tell me it was all wrong."[29] She later learned that Berryman praised her effusively: she was among "the best students I ever had."[30]

Dogged, DeFrees ignored her dissenters and kept writing. She documents her typical process of composition during a scene in *The Springs of Silence*. She had recently experienced a dry season of faith, and had joined fellow sisters in Gearhart, Oregon, where the Sisters of the Holy Names owned a house on the beach. Some sisters hiked trails or searched the nearby woods for berries; DeFrees instead chose to relax on the beach with some like-minded peers. "A facetious stranger walking up the beach," she joked, "might have mistaken us for penguins, so much a part of the landscape we had become."[31]

Some on the beach read, others prayed. DeFrees "did nothing." Instead, the "endless rhythm of the surf stole into my consciousness, healing the tired mind and quickening the latent love for poetry." She gave herself over "to the mysterious power of wind and wave," and began to look differently at the surrounding landscape. Craggy driftwood on the beach now "looked like distorted dreamscapes; grotesque, but somehow shorn of their fearfulness."[32]

An idea arose from the images: "One had to learn to look at her own capacity for evil; to face the depths to which human nature, divorced from God, might descend. The corollary was, of course, the heights to which she could rise with the help of God's grace." She thought of the poem's first stanza: "On this sandy point the seeker / May conquer the obdurate sea / And learn from her chastened waters / That one humility."[33] The full poem was later published in *Spirit* in January 1949.

DeFrees continued to write of nature and landscapes. Unsurprisingly for a poet forged in the Pacific Northwest, DeFrees depicts snow and silence, as in "Early Winter": "The harvest burden bent the crusted branch / Serenely to the earth until it brushed / The snow with color, and reluctance rushed / To free its treasure in an avalanche."[34] Similar imagery returns in "Signals": "Strung on magnetic frequencies / In aureoles of dance, / The incandescent snowflakes / Suffuse our small pretense. // Bewilderingly simple / And born to last a breath, / They range the tall uncertainties / To how sublime a death."[35]

From the Darkroom is steeped in the imagery of trees. Years later, DeFrees would note: "I used to watch trees. I wanted to be like a tree— rooted but moving."[36] In "Tree for Cremona," she writes: "On the dark side of a mountain / upon high ground where roots wound / stubborn as tentacles in the storm-flung foam, / each winter the old tree held."[37] In "Recession," on a cold morning, fruit falls "between the orchard rows" in "a late warning / Of what the lean branch knows."[38] DeFrees's arboreal sense was preternatural, as if her syntax rode the sinew of branch and trunk. "Gestures of Autumn" is full of stellar lines: "Planed smooth long before autumn / the sycamore bares bone to lonely stretches, / high above flaked flank and locked limb / her riches shower, indiscriminate lank / clean swatches of clear color / less prodigal than maple."[39] Later in the poem, the tree recalls an exhausted maternal figure: "Skeletal even in her hour of glory, / stripped down without shame / and delivered of pendulous fruit / she anchors her spare form / to the wide wounds and ponderous spaces / of knife-blue and time-tilted air."[40]

She imbues mythic imagery—with shades of Robert Penn Warren—into "Low-key Landscape": "Their angularity withdrawn, bare boughs limber / in the soundless air, rounding to grace / over suspended lawn, and trace / their legends, indistinct and free. / Pale grasses wear their shadows' signature transparently."[41] As she was rooted in the convent, DeFrees examines the nature of trees as static, our closest bridge to eternity. She begins "Eden Revisited" with a touch of longing: "The Tree of Knowledge blooms outside the cloister door / And rebel eyes stray fondly toward its boughs / Each evening when the slumbering passions rouse / and dally with consent."[42] The poem ends, tantalizingly, on an open note: "The branches quicken / With something less than life as shadows thicken / In gardens set apart, / About the blighted fruit that lightly nods / To hollow breezes sighing '...be as gods...'"[43]

DeFrees also turned her poetic gaze inward, toward the walls of her convent. "Some people seem to think that being a member of a religious order would be restrictive as to writing," she said. "But I don't feel this as far as poetry is concerned. I feel more free than I would be otherwise."[44] "Requiem Mass: Convent Cemetery," is a moving, funereal piece. "Life shrinks to a pair of names / (born into one, the other worn with the veil)." She writes that the "solitary, single hearts" of the sisters were "quickened by the same Love / in a million guises." She ends with a wonderful final stanza: "Disguises, rather, for we seldom see / from above the tombstones. Only now and then / between the Introit and the last Amen, / here in the cemetery, / we look and gauge our place and look away."[45]

DeFrees continues her solemn touches in "Matinal." The narrator wakes at 4:30 in the morning during a "soggy May." "Unbreakable as doom / five street lamps watch me come / to keep my tryst." The lamps are "Nailed each to a man-made cross." The light "hooding our early brightness in a cloud / tempers the shock / and orders lonely emanations / by a clock."[46] Her final end rhyme, the only one in the poem, nicely punctuates the piece.

DeFrees's poems tend to be less outwardly steeped in divine praise than her peer nun-poets, yet they are still distinctly Catholic.

DeFrees, ultimately, is interested in transformation, divine and otherwise. The book's first line comes from the title poem: "The image comes up slowly from where light fell." There appears an image, "pure positive from what was only lack."[47] In "Undertow," the narrator again experiences transfiguration: "Bound to no shore, I sheer and tack, / veer in the wake of wreckage flung."[48]

Commensurate with transformation, and endemic to the Trinitarian vision of Catholicism, lies the necessity and inevitability of paradox. In "Polarities," DeFrees writes: "In all creation opposites conspire / morning and evening for a golden noon: / divergencies at length are reconciled / to intersect like street and avenue. / Antithesis gives way to analogue, / sweeping our neat distinctions into dust."[49]

The poem appears rather autobiographical. In one chapter of her memoir, DeFrees describes a crisis of faith and vocation that she experienced in the convent. One morning, she awoke to see "the moonlight streamed through the small window of my room, lighting the worn floor and the bare walls with unmerciful realism. No illusion left."[50] Morning prayer was no salve. Irritated, she fixated on one sister's faded veil, and another's atonal repetition. The distress continued, and DeFrees was equally frustrated with the annoyances as she was with the break in her quiet, resolved approach to vocation. Other sisters spoke of dramatic struggles of faith. She, who had preferred a more metered approach, now withered.

Days became weeks, and she became "more disconsolate and weary than ever, convinced that mine was a unique struggle, not one to be lightly confided to those who could not understand."[51] She wept during confession. She worried that her provincial superior's support was based on a false sense of DeFrees as resolute. "I tried to imagine what it would mean to readjust to life in the world"; what it would mean to leave the convent.[52] A sister "who returns to the world after long years in the convent usually does so because of instability and not infidelity. Indecision is a far more common factor than disloyalty."[53]

DeFrees stayed the course. She taught, she prayed, she wrote. Yet the spiritual test was no mere aberration; it became an anchor. One line from her memoir, written as conjecture, now appears to have been prophetic: "if the decision to abandon the religious life proceeds from a real unfitness for it, the subject may, and often does, find satisfaction in marriage or in a single life in the world."

* * *

When DeFrees was completing her graduate studies in journalism at the University of Oregon, she often ate lunch in the nurses' cafeteria at the nearby Sacred Heart Medical Center, a hospital run by the Sisters of St. Joseph. Afterward she prayed in front of the Blessed Sacrament, and examined her conscience at noon. "The solitude and silence," she wrote, "were even more precious after a morning of crowds and clamor, and I'd try to pack into my fifteen minutes there enough quiet and tranquility to last through the long afternoon."[54] DeFrees always felt the pressure of time: writing, ultimately, was her most perfect form of prayer.

In 1967, DeFrees, "in civilian clothes," accepted a temporary position at the University of Montana, for the poet Richard Hugo, who was in Italy on a Rockefeller Grant.[55] The next year, Hugo returned, published *Good Luck in Cracked Italian*, and became a colleague of DeFrees's. She remained at the university. Six years later, she received a dispensation from her vows from the Sisters of the Holy Names. Some might have thought that her dislocation in Montana spurred the change, but according to DeFrees, the process had begun over a decade earlier, in Bloomington, Indiana, with the brash John Berryman. DeFrees called their time together "the first step in a long journey to discover the buried self."[56]

The two were different, although surprisingly kindred, spirits. Born in 1914 in McAlester, Oklahoma, Berryman served as an altar boy at Holy Family Church in Anadarko. Years later, he wrote of the Benedictine priest he assisted: "I served at Mass six dawns a week from five, / adoring Father Boniface & you, / memorizing the Latin he explained."[57] He attended St. Joseph Academy, a Catholic boarding school in Chickasha, Oklahoma, where he received Communion in the chapel each morning at 6:30 and then returned for Mass at 8:15.

As a boy, he had already felt the sharp pain of loss: his father died by suicide when Berryman was twelve. The memory never left him. In "Eleven Addresses to the Lord," the long poem he wrote at St. Mary's Hospital in Minneapolis, he traced his spiritual wrangling back to that moment, when his father "blew out my most bright candle faith."[58]

Berryman's private correspondence reveals not only his continual shifting between belief and doubt but also that Catholicism remained his point of reference in life. He was drawn to Catholic intellectuals—including the mid-century poets Robert Lowell, Allen Tate, Claude McKay, Kenneth Rexroth (and Rexroth's friend William Everson, who took the name "Brother Antoninus" as a lay brother in the Dominican Order), and Isabella Gardner, among others.

Berryman also admired the work of William F. Lynch, a Jesuit priest who had been the editor of *Thought* at Fordham University. Lynch was the author of a seminal book of literary criticism, *Christ and Apollo*, in which he argued for a Catholicism grounded in the life of Christ rather than in abstractions about God: "Even when the human soul is in the highest of contemplative states—that is to say, when it is locked most securely in the embrace of the timeless divinity—it cannot forego its grip on the humanity and temporality of Christ."[59]

Berryman had read parts of Lynch's book in manuscript around the time that he wrote to the priest that he was having a "religious enquiry."[60] The next day, he wrote Father Lynch again, about the Christian symbolism of a strange dream he'd had about a bar and its bartender: "The 'bar' is the cross-beam, patibulum, in a 'Station' of the Cross; Christ carrying it Himself, bar-tender; but He is also on the Cross, his body 'tender' from the bar, and gives us from it His blood to drink."[61]

These are private musings, not public performances. Berryman clearly had a Catholic center, and yet, like so many Catholic artists, he pushed it away at times. Several years later, in a rather morbid letter to Ann Levine, his second wife, Berryman included a will "in case of fatal accident or death," stipulating: "I die outside the Church, and care very little about the sort of service for burial, except that I do not want any eulogies. If anything is to be read, perhaps the last four sections of Whitman's Song of Myself would do."[62] His sometimes harsh approach to DeFrees existed within a tendency of misplaced passion from a mind and personality stirred by religious visions that became frantic, ambitious art.

He was not the first imperfect teacher to have a significant influence on his students. Berryman was a poet of the highest order who offered DeFrees an arresting model for how faith and doubt subsist each other. Their classroom dissent was an artistic furnace; his "abrasive teaching style," combined with her "need for approval" forged "the sense of independence [she] needed to resolve the conflict between [her] poetic and [her] religious commitments."[63]

Although DeFrees attended the School of Letters as an emerging poet, there were other reasons for her enrollment. In contrast to her earlier conception of silence as a calming and focusing element of convent life, DeFrees had begun to feel uncomfortable in her own skin. "I could barely hold my body in place during the half-hour of morning meditation in the chapel," she wrote, "and I imagined myself rising to shatter the silence with a piercing scream."[64] Her gynecologist began treatment but advised "a complete change of scene" out of the convent—and into the poetry classroom.[65]

Despite their superficial differences, DeFrees and Berryman had similar poetic influences, and one formidable Jesuit in common. One of Berryman's great Catholic pieces was "Eleven Addresses to the Lord." In June 1970, he sent his editor, Robert Giroux, a new table of contents for his forthcoming book, *Love and Fame*, to include the "11-lyric new religious sequence that ends the book (written in hospital after a sort of conversion-experience I'll describe to you sometime)."[66] He soon told *Life* magazine reporter Jane Howard that "my relation with Him is quite strong at present."[67] That relation is reflected in his passionate, probing lines: "Holy, as I suppose I dare to call you / without pretending to know anything about you." Berryman, the sinner beset by doubt, wails: "Who am I worthless that You spent such pains / and take may pains again?"[68]

If the roll and rise of these lines sounds familiar, that is for good reason: They evoke the prosody of Gerard Manley Hopkins, the Catholic poet exemplar for Berryman. What made Hopkins both difficult and brilliant, Berryman thought, was "the union, in his finest poems, of vigour & fatigue, confidence & despair, the elegant & the blunt, the bright & the dry."[69] If he felt the occasional swells of joy, Berryman identified only too well with Hopkins's despair. In a letter in 1960, he wrote, "I have not been depressed, but hopeless; in pain at both ends, but chiefly the state wd be best described in Hopkins's words during his terrible last years in Ireland, 'weakness' and 'melancholy.'"[70] DeFrees had "read, memorized and meditated" on Hopkins's poems throughout her novitiate.[71] At first, she tried to imitate his style but soon learned his singular prosody was better for inspiration than emulation. Still, Hopkins showed DeFrees that a poet consumed with God might experience a winter world.

After receiving her dispensation from religious vows in 1973, DeFrees felt freer to write "without the subconscious censorship I had imposed upon myself as a nun."[72] During her time as a sister, poems were an unhealthy paradox; they were her "lifeline because they provided a measure of release for my feelings," yet the desire to write created a perpetual sense of guilt.[73]

Her second collection of poems, *When Sky Lets Go*, appeared several years after her return to secular life, but includes work written during her time as a religious. In ways both practical and metaphorical, the book demonstrates that much of her life as a poet was a time of gestation, a concept she describes in a later essay, "The Radical Activity of Writing Poems."

"No matter how hard one may try to reproduce in language the way a poem springs into the light," she begins, "much of its growth is tuberous: like that of the common potato, a major portion of its steady accumulation is underground and in the dark."[74] She compels writers to move past "the myth of the heavenly muse," and embrace more earthy metaphors: "my task is to prepare the right conditions for growth and to *protect* the germ from those forces that might destroy it before harvest."[75]

This poetic—we might even call it prayerful—cultivation is slow, and is a process of "tending and caring," which "involves energy, sacrifice, work, solitude, quiet."[76] Each poem, DeFrees mused, "always takes all our lives to that point," perhaps an unconscious play on Robert Frost's observation that poets accumulate experience and knowledge like burrs while walking in fields.[77] DeFrees wrote that the first task of a poem is "to keep up with the rapid flow of ideas, phrases, images: a chaos of impressions, only a few of which will find their way into the finished draft."[78] She knew that if "judgment" in the form of editing and revision "enters too prominently into the process too early, it will stop the flow."[79] Yet what must follow is a painstaking reconsideration, a word-by-word assessment of sound and sense that prefaces the poem ever being shared with a reader or editor.

DeFrees experienced that process during her time as a sister and she continued it in her secular life, so that poetry is both the constant force in her existence, and yet invariably affected by her circumstance. For that reason, her first book after being released from vows is perhaps the most salient for understanding her identity as a nun-poet.

"Mexican Crucifix," which originally appeared in *The Sewanee Review* in 1966, opens with a single-sentence line: "The body is its own cross." Its wisdom resides in its truthful simplicity, the Christ shape a source of divinity, humanity, and also punishment. Above his head is "a brier crown" woven "of silver wire," while "silver slants toward / the bent knees, relaxed / and reverent together, as if / suffering were more than a posture." Whether upright on a wall or prone on a table, "the figure / retains its simple lines" with "three rivets for support / and chained to the dark decades."[80]

Christ via the crucifix, that presentation which captivated Catholic artists from Ernest Hemingway to Toni Morrison, is theatrical action. The bare cross offers a shadowy solemnity: the absence of the body a funereal reminder of death and resurrection. The crucifix is body, blood, pain, performance: the suffering is unavoidable, and patently present tense. In her short poem, DeFrees manages to capture the paradox that a crucifix always seems to be mid-movement, however still.

The poetic effect arises from DeFrees's masterful syntax, and is on display in other poems from the collection. "Baroque Lament," another poem written during the mid-1960s, opens with a tantalizing first stanza: "Thistle. The name bleeds on the tongue / and the sessile leaves deny the curious / a handhold. These weeds are nature's mourning / for the unreclaimed."[81]

The affirming confidence of that single-word first sentence is buoyed by the playful yet sharp *st* sound, which DeFrees partially revisits in *bleeds* and *tongue* before fully simmering in *sessile*. *Mourning*, and perhaps even *handhold*, feel like heavy words in the midst— their gravity anchoring the surrounding play. *When Sky Lets Go* puts DeFrees's playful vision on full display; it is as if the poem "Night Driving" is a confession: "My voice, sentenced for fifty years / wants to get out."[82] The spirit of exodus is captured in "Everything Starts with the Fall," set around the time of Michaelmas: "Everything falls from grace: / stars, empires, shadows. / I move in the swordlight play / of that downward journey."[83]

The collection includes a sequence of "blue nun" poems, apparently inspired by a gift of the eponymous wine from her department chair at the University of Montana.[84] In the final poem of the sequence, the narrator makes a salacious announcement: "Sisters, / The Blue Nun has eloped with one / of the Christian Brothers. They are living / in a B&B Motel just out of / Sacramento."[85]

Elsewhere, the collection directly reckons with the life of a woman who has left religious life for domestic spaces and expectations. In "The Family Group," the narrator contemplates life as a woman without children: "That Sunday at the zoo I understood the child / I never had would look like this: stiff-fingered / spastic hands, a steady drool and eyes in cages / with a danger sign." She "wanted to take his hand, / hallucinate a husband."[86]

Several of the late poems in the collection appear to be about her mother. "The Forgiveness" is a complex recognition that the life her mother had hoped she would sustain—the life of a nun—had met its necessary end: "Our tears can run together now. I am not afraid / to let you see them. We call each other across / a narrowing chasm, fear our private line. / I do not have to hide the poems."[87] These modulations of tone and subject reveal a poetically and spiritually mature writer.

DeFrees continued to teach at the University of Montana until 1979, and would later go on to direct the MFA program in Creative Writing at the University of Massachusetts, Amherst. She was a Guggenheim Fellow in Poetry for 1981–82, and published several more collections, including the lauded *Blue Dusk: New & Selected Poems*, which nabbed the prestigious Lenore Marshall Poetry Prize and the Washington Book Award.

Her spiritual concerns remained. During her Guggenheim fellowship, she leased a house in Cannon Beach, Oregon, near the Pacific Ocean. She sought solitude, and thought of no better place than "winter by the sea."[88] Her poems composed there—in a silent personal convent, of sorts—are deeply spiritual. She begins "Power Failure": "Walking the shore, Augustine hoped to comprehend / the mystery: darkness welling up to fill / a small depression hollowed out of sand." The narrator, "fond of light—and secrets" understood "the impulse: the will to know, the wish to be / turned back."

Blue Dusk, in fact, begins with an aptly titled poem: "Going Back to the Convent." "This time it is no dream," the narrator writes. She stays the night there, on apparent retreat, and, "Holy or not, I / feel more at home than in thirty-eight / years I lived here." She wonders: what was her younger self "running from / or into?" Was it a sense of guilt about senior prom, or her mother's wishes for a pious daughter? "Whatever it was," she accepts, "it will soon / be over. I write this now to reclaim it."[89]

Reclamation is a powerful poetic mode. It requires both recognition and naming, coupled with the belief that language is a potentially ample vehicle of documentation. Madeline DeFrees is the only nun or sister in *The Habit of Poetry* to be released from her vows. In some ways, her literary life mirrors that of her contemporary: the fiction writer John L'Heureux.

"I don't know why I became a Jesuit," L'Heureux confessed at the start of *Picnic in Babylon: A Jesuit Priest's Journal, 1963–1967*. "I became a Jesuit, paradoxically, on the grounds of coldest reason: I felt God wanted me to, I could, and therefore I should. So I did." He admitted that "in the past fourteen years I have regretted it often; still, I am aware it is one of the few sensible decisions I've ever made. I rejoice in it."[90]

We can hear L'Heureux's hesitations; his self-dialogue in the recursive syntax. L'Heureux was laicized in 1971, got married, and began a rewarding life of writing and teaching. That later life does not neuter his earlier words; it sharpens them, imbues them with mystery. DeFrees, in her way, rejoiced in the religious gifts of her time as a sister, while also recognizing there was reclaiming work to be done.

4

SISTER MAURA EICHNER:
KENOTIC TEACHER

FLANNERY O'CONNOR'S PERSONAL library included a short book titled *The Word Is Love*, published in 1958. The volume collected thirty poems, divided into three sections: "The Secret," "The Child," and "The Cloister." The book was signed by the author: "For Flannery O'Connor, who knows by what mysterious ways God speaks His word. Sister Maura."[1] Several years later, in a letter to a friend, O'Connor wrote about that author. "The one who runs the writing program at Notre Dame of Maryland is Sister Maura, a poet. As poets, when they are good they are very very good and when they are horrid—she is good."[2]

O'Connor's wit barbed her letters; she cast aspersions and dismissals as often as she invoked the Lord. Her sharp-tongued assessment of some nun-poets might seem harsh but it was shared by the same woman whose work she praised. In 1959, Sister Maura Eichner (1915–2009) gave a speech to the Catholic Poetry Society of America at the Commodore Hotel in New York City. *The Word Is Love* was her second book of poetry and she had been placing verse in both religious and secular publications. Eichner said that most poems by her fellow nuns and sisters were "thin pieties," not "flaming the good tidings of the Incarnation."[3]

The problem, according to Eichner, came from what these nuns would read themselves: the poetry made available to them in convents and schools. She said they read "gilt-edged, moral-weighted verses in spiritual books, ladies' books and memory books of all kinds." Unsurprisingly, she concluded, these women poets "tended to gather decorously sweet nosegays for the lyric basket." Their verses were trite, "derivative and mediocre—rarely, if ever, the work of a great Christian poet."[4]

She acknowledged that her fellow women religious were oversubscribed with responsibilities: "When a sister writes, it is a gloss on the narrow margin of time left over." She was thankful that some poetry from nuns and sisters had become "sometimes competent, sensitive, felicitous," yet she longed for more work created "with the humility of a craftsman and the ardor of a saint."[5]

Sister Maura Eichner's words echoed sentiments from Sister Mary Madeleva Wolff, Madeline DeFrees, and other nun-poets of her generation. These women were acutely aware of the stereotypes of nuns as staid, regimented, and interchangeable. Assumptions of uniformity exacerbated criticisms of their personalities, not to mention their art. While fellow Catholic woman Flannery O'Connor was crafting arresting, violent, and faith-haunted work, literary nuns tended to trade style for piety. Eichner's impassioned speech came from a sense of artistic duty, perhaps, as much as it arose from a sense of pride: she longed for a verse from nuns that could give "glory to God and joy to men."[6]

Beyond the well-honed critical eye of O'Connor, Eichner was praised by her peers. "I tried all of the nun poets," DeFrees said in an interview, "and the one that I liked the best was Sister Maura." DeFrees described Eichner as one who "wrote mostly satirical poems about advertising," which "wasn't exactly my subject." Although their work was dissimilar, she found Eichner's voice to be singular. DeFrees's comments are based on a sequence of poems of Eichner's that appeared in the same issue of a magazine as hers. Although the generalization of her subject matter isn't quite correct, the sentiment is well taken: Sister Maura Eichner was a unique voice.[7]

Born Catherine Alice Eichner in Brooklyn, New York, on May 5, 1915, her childhood was marked by tragedy. Her mother died when Eichner was less than a year old. Her father soon remarried, but his wife deemed young Catherine "a terrible little thing," and sent the child to live with extended family in a railroad flat.[8] "I was always a little startled, then beguiled, by the sound of my Irish grandfather's voice," she recalled. "The brogue was rich and the inversions magical. Like so many children in the New York city school that I attended, I had a German grandfather who sang Bavarian songs to me."[9] The various ethnic traditions of her family were a direct example of how language hewed close to culture, and how storytelling could be lifted by intonation and style.

Young Eichner was also steeped in poetry. One uncle read Alexander Pope's *The Iliad* and *The Odyssey* aloud to her: "I didn't understand anything he was talking about, but I loved it."[10] Eichner would later describe her childhood surroundings as "an urban *Our Town*. Everything happened here: the pain and joy of growth and change, the dailyness of life, birth, love, death, the season's wheel."[11]

At seventeen, she worked as a secretary for the future founder and first president of the American College of Nurse-Midwives, Hattie Hemschemeyer, at the Lobenstine Midwifery Clinic, which supported pregnant women and midwives.[12] She enjoyed the work, but a year later another loss wounded her. Her aunt, "who had been my mother since the day my own mother had died," passed away. Eichner remembered how it felt to stand "between the tall candles in the heavily fragrant funeral parlor looking down at her thin, gentle face; at the hair, grey-white, that swept up from her forehead and from the carved-out temple hollows where the blue veins had grown large and almost translucent in the last months of pain." Unconsoled by words from fellow mourners, Eichner wrote that "no one could understand. Not this kind of loneliness; not this aloneness in the midst of so many people."[13]

Afterward, Eichner thought of a tongue-in-cheek comment from the Sister Superior of her grade school: "If you do not give yourself to God now, you will begin to think you have met the right man."[14] She decided to dedicate her life to God, influenced by her childhood spent at the Church of St. Ignatius, and her education at St. Joseph's School, where the School Sisters of Notre Dame formed her vision of Christian service. Eichner entered the order in 1933.

When she revisited those moments years later, Eichner entered an anaphoric remembrance: "On our clothing day we came to the altar again and again: to receive the heavy bundle of habit and cincture, coif and wimple; to receive the white veil of the novice; to receive the crown of lilies and roses; to receive the crucifix; to receive our new names."[15] She was a woman transformed; even the manners of her order "seemed to lift me out of time and place me in the measureless now of God."[16] Yet her optimism was tempered by pain. "I could not seem to lift my soul above the heaviness of habit and veil," she lamented.[17] The beauty of the world "could never find me now, swathed as I was in my cocoon of linen and serge, of custom and decorum."[18] She told no one, but resigned herself to a personal truth: "If this was what God wanted me to do, He would tell me. If it were not, He would indicate that, too."[19] Eichner accepted the call of God's will, despite her own doubts of commitment. "I realized that there was little of the heroic about me," Eichner said. "I decided to give God the only thing that seemed within my possibilities. I promised to give Him service with joy."[20]

After teaching younger students at St. Mary Academy in Annapolis and Notre Dame Preparatory School ("It was impossible," she wrote. "It was wonderful."),[21] Eichner joined the English faculty at the College of Notre Dame of Maryland in 1943, and remained there for the next fifty years.[22] Her teaching was generative for her poetry, and formative for her identity. By all accounts, she was a uniquely generous and skilled teacher, an inspiration for her students. In a 1965 essay about teaching Dante, she wrote that great literature was transformative for college students. Her students "became poets in talking about a poem. The great work gave them momentary greatness in communion."[23]

For Eichner, teaching was inextricable from her religious vows. She called for fellow educators to have faith "in the greatness of teaching as a vocation. Have faith in your students."[24] She hoped that her students "will be more human" from reading literature; that they might "develop a view of life that can accommodate loss and suffering, an awareness that love almost always calls for self-sacrifice, an ability to be joyfully surprised by a single flower of the horse chestnut tree, a reverence for words."[25] As a teacher, she had been "scared, exhilarated, outraged, humbled, illumined. I have not been bored."[26]

Among her many roles as teacher was that of play director. "Drama," she wrote, "is an imitation of an action by persons who give you a chance to see a small part of life in its wholeness for a little while, so that you will know that life itself is still the greatest miracle of all."[27] Her students performed *Adam*, a twelfth-century Anglo-Norman play, recently translated by Rev. John W. Doyle. Eichner was pleased with the result, and felt that medieval plays could benefit students in unique ways: "from our roots we are still nourished, that in our roots our strength may be found."[28] Modern students are "sensitive to the faith of [their] fathers" when dramatized through performance.[29]

Eichner, like many great teachers, was anchored by her sharp sense of humor. When asked if she used the Bible as a model for writing, she responded: "It's such a fine piece of literature that I think we probably should, but we don't. As a matter of fact, we use the *New Yorker*."[30] In a poem titled "Explication," she quips: "Making a gloss on the text / this far I humanly go: / I understand the first word only / in *Waiting for Godot*."[31] On a more earnest note, Eichner sought to carry forth an educational lineage that she inherited: in her poem "What My Teachers Taught Me I Try to Teach My Students," she intoned: "Make routine / a stimulus. Remember // it can cease. Forge / hosannas from doubt."[32]

In mid-century American Catholic intellectual culture, the university was the site of much literary attention and debate. Writing for *America* magazine, Edward P. J. Corbett, a professor of rhetoric at Creighton University whose *Classical Rhetoric for the Modern Student* would later become a mainstay of composition courses across America, affirmed that "most of the new [Catholic] creative writing and some of the best of it is coming from our campuses—from faculty members and students on those campuses."[33] Corbett focused on the *Atlantic*

Monthly 1955–56 Literary Contest for College Students. "Out of
the fifteen top winners," Corbett observes, "students from Catholic
colleges took seven places." These winners "came from only fifteen
Catholic colleges," and save for one school, those colleges were all *"girls'
schools taught by nuns."*[34]

Corbett's use of italics was meant to capture incredulity: there
was not "a single winner from a Jesuit school or from any of the
larger all-male or coeducational Catholic universities," a trend that
continued from the previous year's *Atlantic* contest.[35] Corbett's conclu-
sion was clear: "if there is any vigorous creative activity taking place on
our Catholic campuses, it is all taking place at our smaller liberal-arts
colleges for girls."[36] In the spirit of charity, I take Corbett's incredulity
to be of scope rather than expectations of gender; the women's colleges
had smaller populations, fewer faculty and staff, and a fraction of the
endowments and resources of the larger Catholic schools. He was
likely aware that Sister Maura Eichner, whose students at the College
of Notre Dame of Maryland took twelve places in that year's compe-
tition, was herself regularly publishing in the nation's most prestigious
literary magazines.

Eichner cultivated a remarkable literary culture at the college:
during her tenure, Notre Dame of Maryland students won a dizzying
297 awards in the annual *Atlantic* magazine student writing contests,
including first-place prizes.[37] She mentored poets by encouraging deep
reading, contemplation, and aphoristic, yet plainspoken, wisdom: "If
you spend half an hour writing down an emotional high, don't think
you have a finished work."[38] In 1986, she was awarded the Theodore
Hesburgh Award for Excellence in College and University Teaching, a
prestigious recognition that led the college to create a named fellow-
ship in her honor. Eichner said her work as a teacher was a form of
motherhood; a life spent forming women in literature and faith. She
addressed her current and former students at the end of a speech in
honor of the endowment: "I have borne you all, and I keep you in my
heart."[39]

However they appreciated her instruction, Eichner's students likely did not fully grasp the deep talent of their humble teacher.

* * *

In 1952, as part of the Gallery of Living Catholic Authors' continuing celebration of its members, French philosopher Jacques Maritain was awarded best nonfiction book of the year for *Man and the State*. After bemoaning a request for him to speak about the "Apostolate of the Pen," Maritain expounded on the "immediate task and purpose" of Catholic writers.[40] Although by nature of their beliefs, Catholic writers seek to spread "divine truth," such desire is "a matter of inner inspiration," not an outward function, since we "would risk spoiling many precious things if we let any kind of utilitarianism, even for the noblest purposes, enter the sphere of art or of speculative knowledge."[41] Catholics must write for the wider world; the "very effort to universalize the expression, to keep from using a too domestic Catholic vocabulary, helps a Catholic writer to be more profoundly faithful to the exacting purity of Catholic truth."[42]

Maritain acknowledges that his artistic vision is challenging. He warns writers of faith about "yielding to the spell of art or human knowledge" rather than remaining focused on their spiritual goals. Conversely, he worries that pious writers use assumptions of shared "divine truth" to "compensate" for a lack of skill and style. The only way to avoid these dual pitfalls, Maritain argues, is "a good deal of humility" and "appreciation of, or yearning for, the ways of the spiritual life."[43]

Maritain's speech first appeared in print in *America* magazine. Either by shrewd editorial placement or curious coincidence, directly after his speech appeared a poem by Sister Maura Eichner. "Lesson from the Ancrene Riwle" is a skillful poem of tradition and sisterhood. It is exactly the type of work imagined by Maritain.

Eichner begins her poem with an epigraph from the titular *Ancrene Riwle*, a thirteenth-century anchoritic text meant to cultivate in its readers a sense of asceticism and penance, as well as tacit awe for Christ's suffering and sacrifice. "In a shield there are three things," Eichner quotes, "the wood, the leather and the painting. All these were in the shield: the wood of the rood, the leather of God's body and the painting of the red blood that made Him fair."[44]

In the lines that follow Eichner's excerpt, the narrator speaks to an intended audience of anchoresses about how "this shield, that is, the crucifix," elevated in the church, becomes a constant reminder: "His beloved should see by it how he bought her love, letting his shield be pierced, his side opened to show her his heart, to show her openly how deeply he loved her, and to draw out her heart."[45]

The narrator of Eichner's poem ponders her "sister-over-centuries" who "read in her rule" while "walled within that anchorhold as keys / could never lock."[46] However different and distant, Eichner feels a kinship with her predecessor. The poetic act of imagination, then, is a patently spiritual exercise: "anneal my song with platitudes; anoint / my lips with pieties of fiction-nun."[47] Eichner, of course, was neither a contemplative nor an extern, a nun who exits her cloister for certain responsibilities; she was a teaching sister. We might perceive hints of both wonder and lamentation in her lines: "Not by a chancel will my door be cut, / who chose this seeming mill-run, stolid way / of making mercy out of labor, shut / by neither grate nor grill from every-day."[48]

In one poem, Eichner, via her narrator-self, manages to both romanticize her anchoress predecessor, while also find palpable inspiration in the hagiography: "God, thong me to the rood, contrive the tether / to bind me to this blood-scraped, beaten leather."[49] She encapsulates one particular tension of these mid-century American nuns and sisters: their inheritance of a significant spiritual tradition that has not always valued their ambitions, literary or otherwise. Although not a contemplative, Eichner was also not quite a *literary* extern. She and her fellow religious were cloistered even in the pages of publications they frequented.

One example was a special issue of *The Literary Review*, a quarterly magazine published by Fairleigh Dickinson University in Madison,

New Jersey. Founded in 1957, the magazine's first issue featured work by John Ciardi, E. E. Cummings, Donald Hall, Langston Hughes, recent Nobel Prize winner Gabriela Mistral, and a local doctor named William Carlos Williams, whom the editors thanked for "his neighborly support in the launching of this *Review*."[50]

The Summer 1966 issue of the magazine included a special section, "Poems by Priests and Religious": Raymond Roseliep, Sister Maura Eichner, Sister Mary Jeremy, Sister M. Sebastian, Sister Mary Gilbert (Madeline DeFrees), Daniel Rogers, Peter Levi, and Thomas Kretz. Kretz, a Jesuit novitiate, curated the section and included a measured prefatory note. "I do not present exclusively the finest religious poets nor the best poems of each poet, but all of the selections are, I think, good poems by poets who have integrated the flesh and the spirit," he wrote. Rather than residing in "ivory towers," the religious poets collected here were concerned with the world: "each is vitally concerned with the wrap of flesh and does not try to prescind from it."[51]

Kretz's usage of "flesh" serves a dual role here: these religious poets wrote of the senses and of bodies, and they did so in a literary world that transcended their religious sphere. This is Maritain's vision of the Catholic writer, and one shared by Eichner herself, who wrote a series on the development of the Christian writer for *Today, National Catholic Magazine*, a publication of Loyola University, Chicago. In one column, she shared how a fellow teaching sister of Notre Dame, Sister Mary Hester, visited her college and told students "not to write about Our Lady until they had first tried to write about a bowl of oatmeal, not to write about love in springtime until they had written about the kitchen stove." The "oatmeal and stove," Hester warned, "will bring to the mind probably fewer cliches."[52]

Eichner agreed, advising young writers to "listen to the silence and look upon the world with wonder and with reverence. Then we can talk about craftsmanship."[53] Eichner could be as wry as Myles Connolly, but perhaps gentler: a teacher's touch. At least to get her charges started: "Begin baldly, dully, if necessary, but begin."[54] Being compelled, driven to write is a refrain in her columns; she told young writers that once they were "released from other work that had to be done"—almost certainly an allusion to her own religious life—they must move "back immediately to the work of writing, the way a compass needle shivers into place due north—always."[55]

Writing, for Eichner, exists "for the pleasure, the intellectual joy, the increased humanness" of readers.[56] Yet she concluded her final column of literary advice with a call to action: "Neither have we produced any novelist of extraordinary stature, and not many of any stature at all. It may be your vocation to be a Christian writer. Begin with courage, humility, perseverance, craftsmanship. And begin now."[57]

Her own poetry was rangy, surprising, and clever. A half-page ad from the publisher Macmillan in the May 25, 1946, issue of *America* noted "Publishing in these days is apt to be a bit hectic, what with the paper shortage and some bad bottlenecks at the printers and binders." Yet one bit of good news was the arrival of Eichner's debut book *Initiate the Heart* which "has an imprimatur": approval from the church that a work by a member of a religious order may be published, and a nod to the magazine's Catholic readership.[58]

Devotional works and biblical recastings certainly numbered among her oeuvre. "I think I am a sister," she recalled upon considering her entrance into the convent, "because God can use any instrument, no matter how ungainly or dull, because God can use anybody, no matter how inconsequential or unprepared, if only the instrument will remain supple in His Hand."[59] Her instrument was poetry. "What we women know. / And how much we keep / within the heart, secret / as the honeycomb that is / your skull growing in me," she writes in "Dialogue at Midnight: Elizabeth to John." Rather than a monologue, Eichner chooses a dialogue between Elizabeth and John the Baptist—although he is still in her womb—and it is a masterful choice. She ends the poem with beautiful language: "My son John, trust this / first solitude. Here in the / ancient cave of my body, / sail inland water / safe from followers, // kings and dancing girls." Eichner suggests that orthodoxy and heterodoxy can exist together, and perhaps sustain each other.[60]

Eichner's Marian poems compelled her readers to consider the nuance of female representations. In works like "Creativity," she is more direct. A camera pans across different rooms of a television writer's home, past him pontificating on his process, beyond "books, books," and finally to his wife, "listening to his words, / hearing— under her swelling smock— / that other life."[61] In works like "Minimal Score," Eichner employs an almost breathless concision as a narrator documents the stuff of junkyards—"bumpers, // tail lights, fenders, / unwound // springs, brake reline"—on his way to reformulating a quote from John Cage: "Purpose / is highest when // it's not any purpose / at all."[62]

Her Marian series illuminates the Blessed Mother, and refracts back onto modern women, inside and outside of the convent. A gentle rhyme is embedded early in "From a Woman's Life": "What Mary knew was just / enough for the usual day: / pull water, flint fire, bake / bread, smile, pray // the dark orations, sleep, wake, / wait." Mary endured pain, but learned "the curve // of living." Her singular life is not without sequel, though, as Eichner sees her in all women: "Each one's journey is a thing // wholly without precedent."[63]

Eichner begins "Born of Mary" speaking of Jesus: his genesis, his body. "Everything made him," she wrote, "soil her sandals slapped, water, / mix of sunlight, dusk, strength, fear, // honey, fish, bread, memories." Eichner's syntax is full of lists and short phrases, a language of accumulation that suggests Jesus was the cosmos incarnate. Eichner ponders how Jesus was the promised messiah, and yet he was also fully human: "alive / and tossed as cattail or bulrush, fear / and faith wrestled—circling her journey."[64]

The humanity of Jesus is central to "Out of Cana,"[65] which builds toward a stunning final stanza. At the end of the wedding, the bride and groom are steeped in love. Full of "sleepy grace," their "guests walked home singing." Others, left behind so as to extend the night, call for more wine. Jesus smiles at his mother. Eichner ends the poem:

"She held his life / as kairos-gift, parting, pain, fulfilling song. // Eat bread. Drink wine. Try to sing the song / of Christ. Live life. If you can dance, dance. / Everywhere grace awaits. Desire to love to love."

This humanity of Jesus arises implicitly in present-day recastings of biblical scenes, as in "Veronica's Veil." The narrator notices the image of a face in her "summer kitchen." Smeared in the juices of fruit, she'd been peeling "silk-suede peaches," but noticed "an image in my palm."[66] The poem is disorienting, charged with the wildness of modern miracle. A similar feeling drives the visceral "Sunday Morning: Migrant Labor Camp." "Urine and feces / smell the chapel / door," where inside the feet of migrants are caked with blood.[67] They sing to the Lady of Guadalupe as "Sun and dust take the altar table." In the balmy, packed chapel, "Jesus waits for that cup / of cold water."[68]

In "Still Life: Waiting," Eichner reaches back to the three visitors from Genesis 18. The narrator writes of her brother, who "sits in the shadow / like old Abraham, ready, / hoping that someone will come // with a message" for his suffering wife. "Sheathed in sheets," she is "skeletal and bald / with the crazed demands // of disease," waiting, much like Sarah, "for three angles to come // with promises of life." Eichner sees grace in those "wild impossible promises"—how the ardent grace of God can be enough to "make her laugh."[69]

"Portents" documents the divine's thunderous arrival, testament to powers beyond our control. Mid-day, "a fanged wind / hurtles garbage cans" while a cardinal darts between branches. The narrator scrapes pigeon droppings from a window while snow makes its way "whining like a dog."[70] Eichner's poems compel her readers to live but to also recognize their errant place in the world, as in "Waiting": "I tell myself: be ready / to be unready. Sate / yourself with nothing: want / nothing more than that. / And wait."[71]

In addition to her 1946 debut, Eichner's books include *The Word Is Love* (1958), *Walking on Water* (1972), *What We Women Know* (1980), and *After Silence: Selected Poems* (2011). Largely absent from her posthumous *Selected Works* volume, though, are her more stylistically acute and original pieces. A sequence of poems that appeared in

The Literary Review in 1966 titled "Suite: University Campus" demonstrates a mostly uncollected shade of Eichner's talent. In the densely packed "Parking Lot," "a fierce cat nurses her brood / in a leaf-logged drain where no one would / park though anyone could." There "four late butterflies detour // over macadam as meadowland"—few could turn a phrase about asphalt with as much song.[72]

Another poem in the sequence considers the South African novelist Alan Paton, whose "words have no sausive / Disneyland rhumba" nor "mock-modest statement." He eschews "cinemascope documentary" instead opting to "speak only of this moment's / harrowing of hell."[73] Despite their different subject matter, the poems are syntactic mirrors: truncated narratives in which phrases are stitched by semicolons and colons, appended with terse, single-word sentences. The mode perfectly fits her poem "Advertising," truly a work of its era: "On the neuter-gender sheath / paint Campbell soup pop art; / blow up breasts and rump / to flip the leering heart."[74] Next: grow out "the beatle hair," don black boots: "shadow the eye; / pluck the eyebrow, tilt the head. / Sell it for cool and high."[75]

In "Mythopoesis," Eichner channels the cadence of newspaper reports to reveal the inadequacy of how we describe and respond to loss. The poem documents the crash landing of United Airlines Flight 859 in Denver, Colorado on July 11, 1961. Started by hydraulic failure while in flight, the plane was thought to have landed safely, before bursting into flames. Eichner captures the eerie, ephemeral calm in her first stanza: "the passengers touched the buckles / of seat belts, and glanced at their traveltight / mouths in the window." Their mirror images disappear in the smoke. Eichner details the destruction, interspersing "strophe" and "epode" into the text, imbuing the crash with cathartic results: "The nation sipped morning coffee with disaster."[76]

Her more stylistic work is no less Catholic than her devotional verse. "When the poet looks at reality," she wrote, "the mystery within it demands reverence and communication."[77] Eichner regularly contributed poems steeped in minutiae and mystery to *Four Quarters*, a quarterly literary magazine published by La Salle College (later

University) in Philadelphia, Pennsylvania. Her work for the publication is syntactically dynamic and even provocative in subject matter. Eichner found a willing audience among other sister, nun, priest, and brother writers in the publication, whose work stood alongside lay and secular contributors.

In "Marginal," one of her first poems for the magazine, she imagines a handwritten confession in Augustine's titular work: "She and I sinned / on the beach at night." In the light of dawn, she remembers Augustine's story of the stolen pear, the "callous stench of fruit, / dredgings of rue." The narrator, guilted, "desires dull," knows "no more white blossoming, / only cull."[78] Eichner revisits the theme of writing and living in the margins in her poem "Of Prophecy," focused on a color drawing in the twelfth-century Lambeth Bible. Her wordplay matches the depth of curiosity: "Caught in the spidery foliage of marginals / locked in the wheels of testament idiom, / prophets and kings with garments loose as rain // and scrolls unwinding like forgotten spools / thrust their collocated fingers toward fulfillment." As she describes the marginal drawing, she embeds parenthetical asides through the text, as if her own language exists within the margins of the poem. Perhaps she, like the anonymous annotator, creates "Line and blur, butterfly tenacity of tendril / interlocking tendril, vernacular of color, / semantics of shadowing instruct the mind."[79]

When Eichner wrote of directly religious subject matter, her lines were profluent, explanatory, and focused. When religion became ground rather than figure—when her subjects were more varied and disparate—her lines became resoundingly stylistic and dynamic. In "Julie," a poem about a college student, she considers the young woman's life in winter and summer. When she travels into the city, she speaks not of the "broken bottles" and "leering whistles," and is instead only concerned about the struggling children whom she tutors: one "boy's eyes were loud as cavities / exposing the nerve." Racism breeds around her as "Klansmen come to town / paunchy in white sheets and Halloween hoods." She finds little solace in church, where she "spoke to a priest lonely as failure." Eichner ends with a melancholic closing: "She only gave this land her death of dreaming, / and came back like Thomas with his hand wet from the wound."[80] Elsewhere melancholy is both prodded and parodied, as in "Woman with Aquarium": "In the fluid world she hobby-created, / there was no stagnancy, no inching pond scum, / no whorl and scream of garbage-inflated // gulls." The woman "forbade dark," even instructing her maid "to purify the water, daily syphoning it from // the tank at regular hours." She populates the aquarium with an "overpaid" cast, including "a prize loach male" to whom she fed "fresh lobster."[81]

Like Madeline DeFrees, Eichner was drawn to the Catholic poet John Berryman. She recalls a reading by the poet in "A Remembrance." Berryman walked out onto stage in front of congregated summer session students, and remained silent. Then he spoke of Anne Frank, who "disciplined herself to get up each morning / as though hope were at the door." "Not since Augustine's *Confessions*," Berryman affirms, had there been "so witnessing a word," leading Eichner to conclude: "Grace is everywhere."[82]

Upon his death by suicide, she wrote "*Dream Songs* Concluded," which ends with haunting lines: "Mercy and truth // are one in the root of the river. // At last I am free. / I am free."[83] In the surrounding years, Eichner had become steeped in considerations of artists, mortality, and bodies in her relationship with the fiction writer Katherine Anne Porter, a Catholic convert. Porter lived in College Park, near the Notre Dame campus, and was recovering from hip surgery. Sister Kathleen Feeley, president of the college, wanted Porter "to be the opening speaker for a series of lectures by prominent women."[84] Porter attended Mass with Feeley and Eichner, and, on the way back from Communion, wept silently.[85] The sisters spent the day before Ash Wednesday in Porter's apartment, where the writer "made French crepes for us, and served them with honey; we drank champagne in tall, crystal flutes."[86]

In 1977, as Porter's health declined after a stroke, Eichner went alone to be at Porter's side. Eichner was moved by how Porter "spoke of and to her right hand, tenderly. She reminded it of all the writing it had done; she reminded it of what good cooking and baking it had done. She felt that she wanted to praise it now, not to disown it when it was helpless."[87] Eichner later wrote a poem about the encounter. "When I came into your room, Beloved," she begins, "your left hand pulled me / down past the paraphernalia / of oxygen tent and mask." Porter spoke of her misadventures, "telling me / that dying will be part / of your answer to the call / that life has been." As Porter pulled back her "bloated / useless writing hand," Eichner "trembled for both of us."[88]

Almost two decades later, Eichner would travel a similar life route. In 1990, she joined several hundred fellow School Sisters of Notre Dame to participate in the Nun Study: an ambitious and comprehensive research program to track the progress of Alzheimer's. Participants consented to regular medical testing, open records, and, upon their death, donated their brains for examination. As of 1998, the sisters were "the largest brain donor population in the world."[89]

Eichner died of congestive heart failure in 2009, at ninety-four years old. She would never be distant from her beloved college, as she requested to be buried at Notre Dame Cemetery, "not far from her longtime office."[90] Former students and longtime colleagues heaped well-earned praise upon her, but Eichner had long thought about her passing; she spoke of a "healthy respect" for death.[91] In her poem "Suggestions for a Nun's Obituary," she advises that upon the death of a sister, we be "brief with eulogistic speech" and "cautious of the gospel of her calvaries." Armed with the self-effacing tone that powered her most parodic and stylistic verse, Eichner concludes: "In her no radiance could be seen: / ember and ash, but rarely fire. / Write this: God loved her, and / greatly she desired to desire."[92]

Throughout her life, Eichner wrote her ideas in black notebooks. As with fellow nun and sister poets, her creative work had to be pushed between myriad responsibilities. Yet she continued to write; she was born a poet. In one of her last scrawlings, Eichner wrote: "One writes poetry in order to find God."[93]

CONCLUSION

Sister Mary Francis: The Habit of Perfection

"OH THE VERY interior life of a Mother Superior / Is not so interior / It's veiled hysterier," belted a nun in *The Complaining Angel*, a musical production billed "For Religious Only." With nearly 800 teaching sisters on the Notre Dame campus for a summer session in July 1956, each of the three performances played to packed auditoriums. In full habit, and without a touch of makeup, Mother Felicitas, played by Sister Mary Roman, SSND, lamented "The roofs need repairing / The budgets need paring / The pace is driving me wild. / If I get to heaven it's because I made twenty-seven / First Fridays when I was a child."[1]

The play was a sequel to *Seven Nuns at Las Vegas*, a 1954 farce that depicts when an arthritic nun's prayers for the healing power of a warmer climate sends nuns from their Indiana convent to Las Vegas. Both plays were written and directed by Natalie E. White, a Yale-trained dramatist and professor at nearby St. Mary's College, who taught at Notre Dame's department of speech during the summer. In her new play, a guardian angel trades places with a nun on earth, and soon learns the convent is a place for high drama. The musical's cast, chorus, and fully garbed Rockettes were all played by nuns. The lone male performer is a religious supply salesman who peddles clickers for rosaries—to awaken the prayerful from slumber.[2]

White, a lay person, needed some help with the lyrics for "The Life Interior of a Mother Superior," so she made a pilgrimage to Roswell, New Mexico, to visit the Monastery of the Poor Clares. The convent was a converted farmhouse, white-framed, with a "roguish red roof" that "leaks when it rains."[3] The Poor Clares were cloistered nuns, so White had to speak through a veiled grille with a young nun named

Sister Mary Francis (1921–2006). White had previously commissioned a play about a cloistered nun, titled *Domitille*, from the young nun—who had been adamant that a certain Sister Maura Eichner, SSND, "the poet whose lovely songs have stirred so many hearts," would play the role of Veronica.[4]

Sister Mary Francis was a poet herself. Several years later, her abbess, Mother Immaculata, told her to enter a book contest. "I don't care" what the book is about, the abbess affirmed. "Just win the prize. The roof needs to be fixed." Before she could enter her book in the contest, the manuscript was shown to Frank Sheed, who published it at Sheed & Ward.[5] The roof was soon fixed.

Sister Mary Francis's story encapsulates the literary ambitions of mid-century nuns and sisters: teachers and contemplatives, poets and critics, traditionalists and progressives. Her literary talent and her life might entice us to wonder: did women like Sister Mary Francis and her fellow nun-poets create such work because of the tension between their religious life and their call to write, or did they create *despite* that tension? When one contemporary critic deemed that the weakest moments in the work of a "convent poet" were when "there is more of the nun and less of the poet," was he observing a general truth?[6] Perhaps of more initial concern is what a reconsideration of mid-century American Catholic literature reveals about religious belief and life writ large. Put frankly, why does Catholic literature matter in America?

* * *

American Catholics of the Jesuit tradition, whether by vows, schooling, or sensibility, affirm the power of the daily examen. A nightly prayer, the examen compels us to review our day, and to consider one experience or emotion that might anchor contemplation. The prayer concludes with our hopes for the next day. Such a prayer structure treats life as a story; an unfolding narrative that can be replayed in one's mind. The examen recognizes that we are unable to revise the story of our day, but we are able to closely read its conflicts, characters, and resolutions.

The daily examen is also a form of self-criticism. The prayer can be stifling when approached from an acerbic critical sense; it is easy, and dangerous, to catalog and dissect every misspoken word and imperfect action, to the point where one's esteem and worth feel negligible. The examen is meant to be a concise and precise action of self-examination, and it is best accomplished when we envision criticism as *generative*: a way to experience the self in a detailed, empathetic way.

It should not be surprising, then, that such taking of account was a staple of self-consideration in mid-century Catholic America. Appropriate to its Jesuit pedigree, *America*, a magazine where the women featured in *The Habit of Poetry* regularly published, was the locus of Catholic intellectual examen. The discussion was shepherded in the mid-1930s by Francis Xavier Talbot, a Jesuit priest who would soon become the magazine's editor-in-chief. In a largely favorable review of the book *The Catholic Literary Revival* by Calvert Alexander, SJ, Talbot quibbled with the usage of the word "revival," noting that in America, "we have had, strictly speaking, no revival, no renaissance, no resurgence. We have had no past with which we might link."[7]

Talbot preferred the word "emergence," which was not only more historically accurate, but also valorized—and perhaps put some healthy pressure on—Catholic writers of the present.[8] In the spirit of his pastoral mission as a priest, Talbot lamented that many Catholic writers of the day had become lapsed, although he did not go so far as to claim piety and skill were connected.

When Talbot took the editorial helm of the magazine the next year, one of his first major initiatives was a plebiscite to identify and laud Catholic writers. The project was inspired by Sister Mary Joseph Scherer, a librarian and archivist at Webster College, then a Catholic college for women in Missouri. A member of the Sisters of Loretto congregation, Scherer earned her PhD from DePaul University, and had a special interest in Catholic literature. Her "Gallery of Living Catholic Authors" at the college had begun "as a rather modest attempt to bring the students of the college in closer contact with Catholic writers by displaying their pictures, manuscripts, and letters in prominent places in the library," but grew into the desire to celebrate literary excellence.[9]

Scherer partnered with Talbot and *America* to create the plebiscite, open to readers of the magazine, whose votes would influence the final selections of the Board of Governors of Webster College Library. The magazine received more than 1,500 responses, and the Board's final selections were published in 1936. Awardees included Hilaire Belloc, Jacques Maritain, Sigrid Undset, Monsignor Fulton J. Sheen, Theodore Maynard, and Sister Madeleva Wolff—the only nun or sister on the list. Talbot clearly intended the plebiscite and resulting discussion to get people talking about Catholic literature.

For historian Arnold Sparr, the Catholic literary revival in America was the convergence of three deliberate forces: "a curious mixture of insecurity, protest, and apostolic mission."[10] Similar to Myles Connolly's earlier argument in *America*, Sparr saw "Catholic publicists, teachers, and literary critics" feeling "compelled to prove both to themselves and to their detractors that Catholic intellectual and cultural life compared favorably with that of the rest of American society." Catholic leaders simultaneously wanted a laity to "become more knowledgeable about its faith" so they might defend against detractors. The revival was patently apostolic in nature, with literary and artistic truths anchored in Catholicism seen as "unchanging" and perhaps the only things "capable of saving the world from chaos."[11]

Sparr finds Talbot engaging in a form of "literary imperialism" when he "annexed the English Catholic revival to that of the United States, hoping that American Catholic intellectual and cultural life would grow in stature."[12] Although Sparr criticizes Talbot's apparent willingness to "celebrate any warm body, so long as it was Catholic, received the sacraments, and set words to paper,"[13] he concludes that Talbot's project "represented an authentic attempt to build an American Catholic literary tradition."[14] Although Talbot's "Catholic modesty gave way to Catholic triumphalism," his cultivation of an American Catholic canon was well-intentioned.[15]

In 1955, *Thought*, a quarterly Catholic journal of culture and ideas co-founded by Talbot, published a provocative speech by Father John Tracy Ellis, an esteemed professor of church history from the Catholic University of America. Ellis had originally delivered the speech at the 1955 meeting of the Catholic Commission on Intellectual and Cultural Affairs at Maryville College in St. Louis. *Thought* was the right venue for the speech's wider dissemination; Jacques Maritain, Thomas Merton, Walker Percy, and Karl Rahner, among others, would publish in the journal.

Ellis begins by citing a fellow historian, Cambridge's Denis W. Brogan, who wrote: "in no Western society is the intellectual prestige of Catholicism lower than in the country where, in such respects as wealth, numbers, and strength of organization, it is so powerful." Ellis affirms: "No well-informed American Catholic will attempt to challenge that statement."[16]

Striking a tone that is part Talbot, part Connolly, Ellis argues that the "American intellectual climate has been aloof and unfriendly to Catholic thought and ideas, when it has not been openly hostile, and it places no burden upon the imagination to appreciate how this factor has militated against a strong and vibrant intellectual life among the Catholics of this country."[17] In response, Catholics have sought to be apologists rather than engaging in "pure scholarship."[18]

Ellis cites a recent study by psychologists Robert H. Knapp and Joseph J. Greenbaum, who endeavored to quantify which undergraduate institutions produced graduate scholars of distinction. Ellis lamented the overall showing of Catholic colleges and universities, save for "one bright spot": the data validated "a fairly common opinion that in a number of ways the Catholic women's colleges are in advance of the institutions for men."[19] At a moment when literary Catholics were attuned to a perceived lack of esteem, or even participation, in contemporary letters, their shining hope arose from one particular group: women.

* * *

In "Criticism and Belief: The Life of the Catholic Critic," an essay from *Renascence*, the literary studies journal of Jesuit-affiliated Marquette University, Thomas P. McDonnell spoke difficult truths to his fellow Catholic critics. He worried that "we too often carp and condemn on moral grounds alone, and therefore pre-empt the primacy of the critical act itself; in other words, instead of exploring a work of literature with sympathy and insight, we moralize upon it."[20]

Far from a provincial action, McDonnell imagines criticism to be aligned with a particular worldview. He does not argue that criticism should arise from an ideological position but rather that criticism cannot be prescriptive, nor can it be reductive. Criticism, he argues, is not "a temporary attitude to be taken off and put on again, like a coat, before going in and out of doors," nor is it "an act of mere propaganda automatically dispensed from a preconceived and arbitrary point of view."[21]

Because Catholic critics read from a worldview formed by a moral vision of the world, they are inclined to read *for* and *toward* morality. Such a reading is not immediately negative but it can render the Catholic critic staid. McDonnell is clear: "of all critics, the Catholic critic can least afford a narrow or limited view either of life or of literature, or of those places in art where they virtually become one."[22]

McDonnell edited Thomas Merton's *Reader*, a collection of the priest's writing, so he was acutely aware of how a Catholic writer might enter the mainstream literary world without sacrificing a Catholic identity. In the midst of his essay on Catholic critics, McDonnell shares an anecdote about Henry Rago, the Catholic editor of a resolutely secular magazine, *Poetry*, as a way to demonstrate that the religious and the secular might not be so distant in their search for truth.

Rago, a professor of theology and literature at the University of Chicago, was at a dinner with Herbert Andrew Kenny, the Boston poet and later book editor of the *Boston Globe*. Rago listened to Kenny's decidedly Catholic literary worldview. Kenny argued that critics inevitably have a sense of "absolutes": anchoring ideas for their world-view. Critics whose worldview arises from politics, economics, or the sciences "will invariably assume the rigidities of these categories and that consequently will limit your freedom of range in thinking about them and their relationships to other kinds of knowledge." Kenny, however, argued that a critic instead begins from an anchor of theology, "then you can range infinitely upward in complete freedom."[23]

McDonnell develops Kenny's abstract claim through the work of two Catholic critics: the French essayist Charles Du Bos, and the Belgian theologian and priest Charles Moeller. Both men believed that an authentic religious sense of criticism was neither ideological nor sentimentally spiritual; instead, a religious sense "enriches the vision of the literary world, because it adds supplementary categories of thought, new 'geometric dimensions' in depth, the dimension of grace at the top, and that of sin at the bottom."[24]

In Moeller's commentary on the work of Du Bos, he isolates three traits of a literary critic "incarnated" with a theological anchor: "to *discover* and express the truth of the literary masterpiece," to "*situate* it by *comparing* it with other works," and then "to judge it by *integrating* it into a complete view of man."[25] While such an approach overlaps with the work of secular critics, it differs on several essential points. Both secular and religious critics discover, situate, compare, and judge, yet the Catholic critic's vision of truth is rooted in an incarnational view of the world. The work must never be bent toward this view—and that is the reason for rampant moralizing from Catholic critics—but the work must be enlightened, through critical conversation, by this view. "Literature," Du Bos wrote, "is life becoming conscious of itself."[26]

Although McDonnell did not share Rago's reaction to Kenny's claim about Catholic critics, we can examine the editor's own writing to find his perspective. A few years before starting his tenure at *Poetry*, Rago published an essay titled "Catholics and Literature." Rago is dismissive of a formidable Catholic literary revival in America, espe-cially in poetry. He worried that much of the problem came from the

Catholic *reading* public, whose sentiment influenced the few Catholic publications that reviewed and promoted literature. Mediocrity was the norm, which led to low expectations: "this tendency causes even a good Catholic writer to be praised in grotesque disproportion to his true merit, and at the same time it denies him the professional standards, which, as a matter of both pride and honesty, he would want to be measured by." In its most vulgar form, unbridled praise for average Catholic writing arose from a sentimental source: "this vice would lead one to think that the sacrament of baptism, even when received fairly late in life, forgave not only mortal and venial sins but also faults of style."[27]

Rago's tone and approach needs to be taken in its proper framing and context: he worried that Catholic readers were not intellectually prepared to be honest critics of literary skill, opting for fraternal praise rather than honest response. Although Rago was dismissive of the Catholic literary revival in his seminal essay, it remained a concern in his classroom at the University of Chicago, and in his function as editor of *Poetry*. In his foreword for the fiftieth anniversary issue of the magazine, Rago distinguished between "eclectic" and "catholic" art. Eclecticism, he notes, "suggests an uncertainty about what one really wants, and a settling for bits and pieces of what various people seem to have wanted; it looks like everything but is really not enough of anything and so amounts to nothing." In contrast, a catholic view "implies a sense of poetry as kind of absolute, a center which perhaps no one ever attains but which can be approximated from an unlimited number of possible points of departure, each the only one, desperately the only one, for the poet concerned."[28]

Rago was careful not to directly use a capital C Catholic formulation here, but his own Catholic vision is clear. His editorial vision for *Poetry*, and his broader critical aesthetic, was underpinned by a theological, incarnational view of the world. The poetic center of which he speaks is one anchored in Truth, and his affirmation that poets attempt to seek that Truth without ever capturing it exactly feels patently Christological. It echoes a sentiment from Henri de Lubac, the French Jesuit and theologian: that to be Catholic, "it is necessary to have a mind that is larger than one's own ideas."[29]

* * *

The debate over contemporary Catholic literature had been unfolding for nearly twenty years in Catholic magazines and journals, but it wasn't until 1959 that the debate reached a broader reading audience. *The Saturday Review* boasted a circulation of over 200,000 readers, and would garner over a million dollars in advertising revenue the following year—placing it just under the country's top magazines.

The September 5 issue of the magazine featured an essay by Thomas P. Coffey, an editor and publisher, and teacher of philosophy at Fordham and St. Peter's University. "Is There an American Catholic Literature?" appears to answer its question in the first sentence—with a resounding no—and adds a touch of acerbic humor in the vein of Myles Connolly: Catholic "articles, poems, novels, biographies are, of course, as plentiful as hot dogs at Coney Island. We might add that they are equally indigestible and sometimes even dangerous."[30]

Yet Coffey ends his essay with an optimistic and important paradox. "Catholic literature," he concludes, "ought neither to obliterate man and his world nor to lose touch with God and the spiritual ideals it preaches. For in cutting itself off from these roots of its life, it would betray both the challenge and the promise that it was founded, originally, to impart."[31]

Early in the next decade, Catholic novelists Walker Percy and J. F. Powers would win the National Book Award for fiction in consecutive years. Yet neither writer arose in these frequent debates about the dearth of American Catholic fiction. Similarly, while Catholic intellectuals and editors bemoaned the state of American Catholic poetry, nun-poets were publishing in religious and secular markets, and teaching the next generation of writers. These women, too, remained outside of these largely abstract intellectual debates—save for one important essay.

A few months after he considered the life of the Catholic critic, Thomas P. McDonnell wrote about nun-poets for *Spirit*, the Catholic journal of poetry. Early in the essay, McDonnell laments that "not a single so-called serious critic, to my knowledge, has written on the phenomenon in modern literature of the nun as poet."[32] His assertion is correct. Although single-volume collections by nuns were reviewed in publications, and occasionally paired together in capsule responses, no writer had examined the burgeoning roster of nuns and sisters writing skilled poetry. Nearly sixty-five years later, *The Habit of Poetry* is the first book-length examination of these women as a group, and like McDonnell, I'm surprised to see these talented women ignored.

McDonnell posits three reasons for the rise of nun-poets. First, "many talented and gifted women are going into the religious orders."[33] Following the Sister Formation Movement, convents and women's colleges were spaces where young women exist within an intellectual atmosphere, and are treated as rising scholars. These women form a community in which their lives are arranged by defined and intentional habits, so that "this abundant talent [has] a centrality of meaning." Finally, the faith and inevitable doubt of these women is "a theme, a cohesion of purpose... seldom found in the amorphous mass of so much modern poetry."[34]

McDonnell considers the work of Sister Mary Francis, Sister Maura Eichner, and Jessica Powers. His observation that "most modern critics are simply not equal to the task of exploring the relationship between the mystic and poet" was meant to explain the absence of scholarship on the work of Powers, but it speaks to a broader critical concern.[35] Nun and sister poets are conundrums in an even more acute way than priest poets and the words of Thomas Merton are instructive in this instance.

While the women in *The Habit of Poetry* were publishing their writing, winning awards, and breaking ground in teaching and administrative capacities, Thomas Merton was also a rising literary star— and shared their belief that religious truth could be cultivated through poetry. In his essay "Poetry and Contemplation," Merton argues that true Christian poetry can only be written by those who are "in some degree a contemplative." He clarifies: "All good Christian poets are then contemplatives in the sense that they see God everywhere in His creation and in His mysteries, and behold the created world as filled with signs and symbols of God...the whole world and all the incidents of life tend to be sacraments."[36] Merton knew the contemplative life proper was not for all of those who had committed to a religious vocation. He called for contemplatives "outside the cloister and outside the rigidly fixed patterns of religious life—contemplatives in the world of art, letters, education, and even politics."[37] Ultimately, what was most essential was that Christian poets write with a sense of contemplation—what Merton called the "manifestation of the Spirit," following Paul's first letter to the Corinthians.[38]

* * *

Although Sister Mary Francis's Roswell abbess, Mother Immaculata, saw a utilitarian purpose for her charge's writing, the contemplative nun was a poet at heart. Years earlier, while Mary Francis was still at the Chicago cloister, her aunt sent her verse to the most famous sister poet of the time: Sister M. Madeleva Wolff. Wolff was quite taken with the poems, calling them "among the finest religious poems in contemporary writing."[39] Wolff successfully campaigned on the young contemplative's behalf to her abbess, writing "How I rejoice that this gift of poetry is secure in the cloister" and providing a blurb for her first book of poems.[40] Wolff even made the pilgrimage to Mary Francis's cloister "and sat at the parlor grille with the rapt attention of one who had come to learn."[41] Mary Francis had other literary visitors. The esteemed English writer Hilaire Belloc sent his daughter, Eleanor Jebb, to the monastery to tell Mary Francis: "These poems set bells ringing in my heart."[42]

Her poetry was marked by humor and devotion. In "Apology to a Fly," she wondered if it was "offended that I flailed out left / And right to halt you?" She prayed for patience: "Isaian understanding given, / In that thick moment by your humming riven!" She realized that this work of creation, who spent "spinning your brief life in unstumbling dance," sang not "drone, drone, drone" but "God! God! God!"[43] Her fourteen-section, epigrammatic sequence, "The Stations of the Cross," unfolds with a power reminiscent of William Everson, her contemporary who lived as Brother Antoninus, a Dominican lay brother, for eighteen years. The final section affirms hope: "Sleeping. You sleep / In sepulchre / Sealed with finality. // Restless in death, / I twist and cry // Until You break my heart / To set / Me free."[44]

In the tradition of St. John of the Cross, she wrote of devotion as the deepest love. After quoting the psalmist's call to serve God in fear and rejoice in trembling, she writes: "And fear be all my grace. / My gaiety, Your face / Hid in remotest bliss / Penetrated by my kiss."[45] Elsewhere, as in "Desert Nocturne: Three Responsories," her syntax is deft, managing compression without clunkiness: "Ashes, fetch the ashes for a head / Bowed, proper-bent with sorry history."[46] A pleasant jumpiness infused her prosody: "Solomon needs seeking with a purchase- / Price of fruity-rich solicitations. / Golden ponderings, shekels-conclusions / Before a question's fit for asking."[47] Her lines could be surprising in their juxtapositions, as in "Western Epiphany": "Our hearts are places of narrow corridors / Loud as nightmares, / Busy calculations crawl in our soul / Like ants."[48]

"Act of Contrition," one of her longer poems, employs parentheticals to demonstrate the halting nature of prayer. "If there is something to say, then quickly say it," the narrator admonishes to herself—the first of a series of self-interrogations. She later chastises her own lack of humility, and her idle uses of language to avoid facing her sins head on. Yet she is unable to find the necessary expression, for her "voice is caught in the lonely trees" and she is "pinioned on a point" and "cannot show you" the truth of her pain. The great, lonely work of prayer is perhaps language at its most honest. For much of our public lives, "We draw the pitiable words of civilization / Up like chairs that cannot ever hold us," although "the great mystery of pain hangs over."[49]

Despite her frequent publications of poetry and prose, Mary Francis remained humble because of her order's need to be "servants of all," and her sense of humor.[50] Those who thought that only the "love-lorn and disappointed" and the "neurotic" joined cloisters were sorely mistaken: "Just fancy twenty-five neurotic women rubbing shoulders all the days of all their lives in a cloister. The place would blow up! And the insurance agency could write it up as 'spontaneous combustion.'"[51] Mary Francis first learned the importance of humor while a student at Saint Louis University, when she spoke with a Jesuit priest about the contemplative vocation. At first, he asked if she was prone to ecstatic visions. Nervous, she admitted no, and then he laughed. "Good," he said, and went on to laud "a love for silence and interior prayer,"[52] a sense of humor, and the wisdom to know when to rest: "When you sit on a chair, let the chair hold you."[53]

An ability to laugh was absolutely essential to the religious life: "The ability to see *through* things and to know what is important and what is not, what is to be endured and why we endure it, what is to be tolerated out of compassion and what is to be extirpated out of duty, is dependent upon one's sense of humor."[54]

Following the Second Vatican Council's 1965 decree on the adaptation and renewal of religious life, *Perfectae Caritatis*, Mary Francis found it necessary to clarify misreadings of some passages. Of particular concern to her were statements about cloistered living which "must be adjusted to conditions of time and place and obsolete practices suppressed," including the allowance of exemptions for nuns to "fulfill the apostolic duties entrusted to them." Additionally, the decree called for religious habits to be "suited to the circumstances of time and place and to the needs of the ministry involved," and if not, those habits "must be changed."[55]

Mary Francis lauded the "freshness of challenge and positive change" inspired by the council documents, so she lamented "the wrangling and rebellion and disintegration that are assuredly non sequiturs of Vatican II's intentions."[56] She affirmed the importance of tradition by writing "we have a present only because we have a past. And we build a future only by living in the present."[57] She and her fellow contemplatives "would as soon as take off our skin as our Franciscan garb."[58] She ends poetically: "Leaf-shedding is not an autumnal entity, nor are bare trees a winter totality; both are part of springtime's promise and summer's fruitfulness."[59] The tension over proposed changes inspired poetry from her, as with "Roles Reversal," in which she writes to Saint Clare, her order's namesake: "Forever singing Mother / Hoarse from futile / Lyric, for parched throat / Take my cup of tears." She sees Clare as the church personified, "shabby in torn garment," and promises "I come to mend your vesture / Whole again."[60]

For Mary Francis and the other women featured in *The Habit of Poetry*, the tension between tradition and modernity, between literary ambition and pious humility could by turns be stymying and generative. Their accomplishments call to mind their brother in faith and poetry, Gerard Manley Hopkins, for whom nuns were not merely the subjects of his poems, but symbols of piety. Although "The Wreck of the Deutschland" is a masterwork, two earlier pieces affirm the identity of women religious. In "Heaven-haven," a nun takes the veil: "I have desired to go / Where springs not fail, / To fields where flies no sharp and sided hail / And a few lilies blow."[61] Cloistered in setting but not in her vantage point, hers is the world entire. Likewise, in "The Habit of Perfection," Hopkins encapsulates the paradox of religious life: "Elected Silence, sing to me / And beat upon my whorled ear, / Pipe me to pastures still and be / The music that I care to hear."[62]

The women in *The Habit of Poetry* elected silence and embraced poetry. Madeleva Wolff, Jessica Powers, Mary Bernetta Quinn, Madeline DeFrees, Maura Eichner, and Mary Francis are no monolith. They were women of varying talents, personalities, and regions. Some were contemplatives; others were teachers. Yet all of them were poets. Their poetry was syntactically skilled, stylistically ambitious, and rooted in the paradoxes of belief. These Catholic women wrote and published poetry at a time when nuns and sisters were fighting for respect and support. They published alongside the finest secular poets of their day—and received their admiration. Theirs was an artistic renaissance in mid-century America; a recognition that nuns and sisters could create complex representations of life and love. Their work is significant, and the lives of these nuns and sisters are models for artists who wish to sing of doubt and belief.

NOTES

Preface

1 Denise Levertov, "Cædmon," *Southern Humanities Review* 19, no. 3 (Summer 1985): 203.

2 Quoted in Judith Dunbar, "The Sense of Pilgrimage," *America* 178, no. 19 (May 30, 1998): 24.

3 Denise Levertov, "Work That Enfaiths," *CrossCurrents* 40, no. 2 (Summer 1990): 150.

4 Levertov, "Work," 152.

5 Levertov, 153.

6 Levertov, 158.

7 Although often used interchangeably, the terms "nun" and "sister" connote different religious lives. Nuns are typically clois-tered; sisters profess simple vows and live apostolic lives out in the world. Of the women religious depicted in this book, Hilda, Sor Juana, Jessica Powers, and Mary Francis fit the traditional description of a nun, living a cloistered life.

8 Bede, *Historia ecclesiastica gentis Anglorum (Ecclesiastical History of the English People),* trans. A. M. Sellar (London: George Bell & Sons, 1907), 279.

9 Bede, *Historia,* 279.

10 Bede, 279.

11 Clare A. Lees and Gillian R. Overing, *Double Agents: Women and Clerical Culture in Anglo-Saxon England,* (Cardiff: University of Wales Press, 2009), 26.

12 Levertov, "Cædmon," 203.

13 Paul Mariani, *Gerard Manley Hopkins: A Life* (New York: Viking, 2008), 131.

14 Claude Colleer Abbott, ed., *The Letters of Gerard Manley Hopkins to Robert Bridges* (London: Oxford University Press, 1935), xxiv.

15 Mariani, *Gerard Manley Hopkins,* 155.

16 Abbott, *Letters,* 49.

17 Gerard Manley Hopkins, *Poems and Prose*, ed. W. H. Gardner (Baltimore: Penguin Books, 1968), 12.

18 Hopkins, *Poems,* 16.

19 Hopkins, 17.

20 Hopkins, 19.

21 Hopkins, 20.

22 Kathleen Elgin, *Nun: A Gallery of Sisters* (New York: Random House, 1964), 9.

23 "Journalistic Nun Pursues Studies," *New York Times,* March 29, 1964, 62.

24 Sor Juana Inés de la Cruz, *Poems, Protest, and a Dream: Selected Writings,* trans. Margaret Sayers Peden (New York: Penguin Books, 1997), 190–91.

25 Octavio Paz, *Sor Juana, or, the Traps of Faith*, trans. Margaret Sayers Peden (Cambridge, MA: Harvard University Press, 1988), 1.

26 Sor Juana, *A Sor Juana Anthology,* trans. Alan S. Trueblood (Cambridge, MA: Harvard University Press, 1988), 212.

27 Sor Juana, *Anthology,* 176.

28 Sor Juana, 213.

29 Sor Juana, 218.

30 Sor Juana, 218.

31 Paz, *Sor Juana,* 1.

32 Sor Juana Inés de la Cruz, "You Foolish Men," accessed July 20, 2022, https://poets.org/poem/you-foolish-men.

33 Paz, *Sor Juana,* 499.

34 Sor Juana, *Selected Writings*, trans. Pamela Kirk Rappaport (New York: Paulist Press, 2005), 3.

35 Sor Juana, *Anthology,* 7.

36 Sor Juana, 49.

Introduction

1 "About the Contributors," *Poetry Northwest* 2, no. 3 (Summer 1961): 48.

2 Sister Mary Gilbert, SNJM, "Tumbleweed," *Poetry Northwest* 2, nos. 1–2 (Winter 1960–61): 18.

3 Gilbert, "Nuns in Quarterlies," *Poetry Northwest* 2, nos. 1–2 (Winter 1960–61): 17.

4 Gilbert, "Nuns," 18.

5 Gilbert, 18.

6 Gilbert, 18.

7 Ezra Pound, "Small Magazines," *The English Journal* 19, no. 9 (November 1930): 701.

8 Pound, "Small Magazines," 702.

9 Pound, 702.

10 Pound, 703.

11 Felix Pollak, "The World of Literary Magazines," in *Paper Dreams: Writers and Editors on the American Literary Magazine*, ed. Travis Kurowski (Madison, NJ: Atticus Books, 2013), 159.

12 Pollak, "Literary Magazines," 160.

13 "Announcement," *Four Quarters* 1, no. 1 (November 1951): 1.

14 Richard P. Coulson, "A Further View," *Four Quarters* 5, no. 1 (November 1955): 16.

15 Coulson, "Further View," 16.

16 Coulson, 16.

17 Coulson, 18.

18 Coulson, 20.

19 Coulson, 20.

20 "A Nun Appraises Modern Poets," *Buffalo Evening News*, April 25, 1962, 49.

21 Marya Zaturenska, "Music That Is Peace," *New York Times*, February 15, 1948, BR6.

22 Madeleva Wolff, *My First Seventy Years* (New York: Macmillan, 1959), 147.

23 Gail Porter Mandell, *Madeleva* (Albany: State University of New York Press, 1997), 205.

24 "Nun, President and Poet," *Life*, June 10, 1957, 130.

25 Wolff, *My First Seventy Years,* 3.

26 Wolff, 16.

27 Wolff, 24.

28 Wolff, 26.

29 Wolff, 27.

30 Wolff, 28.

31 Wolff, 29.

32 Wolff, 32.

33 Wolff, 35.

34 Wolff, 45.

35   Advertisement, *The Review of Politics* 17, no. 4 (October 1955).

36   Pollak, "Literary Magazines," 162.

37   Pollak, 163.

38   Peter Michelson, "On the Purple Sage, Chicago Review, and Big Table," in *The Little Magazine in America: A Modern Documentary History*, ed. Elliott Anderson and Mary Kinzie (Yonkers, NY: Pushcart, 1978), 342.

39   Michelson, "Purple Sage," 373.

40   Mandell, *Madeleva*, 54.

41   Mandell, 50.

42   Wolff, *My First Seventy Years*, 105.

43   "Nun, President and Poet," 129.

44   Wolff, *My First Seventy Years*, 146.

45   Wolff, 146.

46. Wolff, 147.

47   Mandell, *Madeleva*, 83.

48   Mandell, 217.

49   Mandell, 217.

50   "Nun-poetess Sees End of Free-verse Period," *Los Angeles Times*, May 7, 1932, A9.

51   Mandell, *Madeleva*, 226.

52   Mandell, 231.

53   Meryle Secrest, "Modern Literature Lacks Old Ideals," *Washington Post*, July 7, 1962, A11.

54   Mandell, *Madeleva*, 216.

55   Madeleva Wolff, *Chaucer's Nuns, and Other Essays* (Port Washington, NY: Kennikat Press, 1965), 21–22.

56   Wolff, *Chaucer's Nuns*, 22.

57   John W. Donohue, "Three Sisters," *America* 180, no. 3 (January 1, 1999): 20.

58   Barbara C. Jenks, "Sister Madeleva and Saint Mary's," *The Family Digest*, September 1960, 33.

59   Mandell, *Madeleva*, 209.

60   Garry Wills, "Women Who Defied Fate," *New York Times*, December 21, 1980, BR1.

61   Wolff, *My First Seventy Years*, 45.

62   "Nun, President and Poet," 129.

63   Wolff, *My First Seventy Years*, 111.

64   Wolff, 111.

65 Sister Bertrande Meyers, *Sisters for the 21st Century* (New York: Sheed & Ward, 1965), 33.

66 Wolff, *My First Seventy Years*, 112.

67 Sister M. Madeleva Wolff, CSC, "The Education of Our Young Religious Teachers," *Bulletin: National Catholic Educational Association* 46, no. 1 (August 1949): 253.

68 Wolff, "Education," 254.

69 Wolff, 254.

70 Wolff, 255.

71 Mary J. Oates, *Pursuing Truth: How Gender Shaped Catholic Education at the College of Notre Dame of Maryland* (Ithaca, NY: Cornell University Press, 2021), 109.

72 Oates, *Pursuing Truth*, 109.

73 Brother Felician Patrick, FSC, "Survey of Responses and Introduction to the Series," *Four Quarters* 10, no. 1 (November 1960): 10.

74 Patrick, "Survey," 11.

75 Brother Felician Patrick, FSC, "Symposium," *Four Quarters* 10, no. 2 (January 1961): 17.

76 Mandell, *Madeleva*, 204.

77 Jack Heher, "Man Seen at His Best 'Thinking About God,'" *Rochester Catholic Courier Journal*, February 28, 1958, 10.

78 Heher, "Man," 10.

79 Sister M. Madeleva Wolff, CSC, *The Four Last Things: Collected Poems* (New York: Macmillan, 1959), 3.

80 Wolff, *Four Last Things*, 13.

81 Wolff, 83.

82 Wolff, 104.

83 Wolff, *My First Seventy Years*, 148.

84 Wolff, *Four Last Things*, 58.

85 Wolff, 58.

86 Wolff, *My First Seventy Years*, 25–26.

87 "Nun-poetess Sees End of Free-verse Period," A9.

88 Wolff, *Four Last Things*, 153.

89 Wolff, 154.

90 Wolff, viii.

91 Mandell, *Madeleva*, 203.

92 Wolff, *Four Last Things*, 20.

93 Mandell, *Madeleva*, 203.

Chapter 1

1 Dolores R. Leckey, *Winter Music: A Life of Jessica Powers: Poet, Nun, Woman of the 20th Century* (Kansas City, MO: Sheed & Ward, 1992), 15.
2 Leckey, *Winter Music,* 59.
3 "Catholic Poetry Society Launched," *The Catholic Transcript,* April 2, 1931, 9.
4 Marianne Kappes CST, *Track of the Mystic: The Spirituality of Jessica Powers* (Kansas City, MO: Sheed & Ward, 1994), 38.
5 Leckey, 94.
6 Kappes, *Track of the Mystic,* 66.
7 Myles Connolly, "Tactics," *America 54, no. 9* (December 7, 1935): 201.
8 Connolly, "Tactics," 201.
9 Connolly, 202.
10 Connolly, 202.
11 Connolly, 202.
12 Connolly, 202.
13 Connolly, 202.
14 Connolly, 202.
15 Connolly, 202.
16 "Who's Who," *America,* April 9, 1938, 1.
17 Jessica Powers, *Selected Poetry of Jessica Powers,* ed. Regina Siegfried ASC and Robert F. Morneau (Kansas City, MO: Sheed & Ward, 1991), 9.
18 Robert F. Morneau, *Mantras from a Poet: Jessica Powers* (Kansas City, MO: Sheed & Ward, 1991), vi.
19 Leckey, *Winter Music,* 33.
20 Leckey, 36.
21 Leckey, 63.
22 Leckey, 48.
23 Leckey, 62.
24 Leckey, 99.
25 Powers, *Selected Poetry,* 102.
26 Leckey, *Winter Music,* 5.
27 Leckey, 105.
28 Leckey, 115–16.
29 Leckey, 115.

30 Leckey, 118.
31 Powers, *Selected Poetry,* 2.
32 Powers, 2.
33 Powers, 10.
34 Powers, 58.
35 Powers, 66.
36 Powers, 66.
37 Powers, 91.
38 Powers, 85.
39 Powers, 50.
40 Morneau, *Mantras,* viii.
41 Morneau, viii.
42 Morneau, viii.
43 Powers, *Selected Poetry,* 7.
44 Powers, 40.
45 Powers, 79.
46 Powers, 94.
47 Powers, 94.
48 Powers, 157.
49 Powers, 157.
50 Powers, 170.
51 Powers, 176.
52 Leckey, *Winter Music,* 92.
53 Powers, *Selected Poetry,* 128.
54 Kappes, *Track of the Mystic,* 73.

Chapter 2

1 Randall Jarrell, *The Complete Poems* (New York: Farrar, Straus & Giroux, 1969), 29.
2 Wallace Stevens, *The Letters of Wallace Stevens,* ed. Holly Stevens (New York: Knopf Doubleday, 1966), 584.
3 Stevens, *Letters,* 584.
4 Stevens, 735.
5 Stevens, 735.
6 Sister M. Bernetta Quinn, OSF, *Design in Gold: A History of the College of Saint Teresa* (Winona, MN: College of Saint Teresa, 1957), 45.
7 Quinn, *Design,* 13.

8 Sister Bernetta Quinn, OSF, *Randall Jarrell* (Boston: Twayne Publishers, 1981), 8.

9 Sister M. Bernetta Quinn, *The Metamorphic Tradition in Modern Poetry* (New York: Gordian Press, 1966), 1.

10 Gege McKay Hodgson, "Mary Bernetta Quinn," accessed July 20, 2022, https://myemail.constantcontact.com/The-Impact-of-Sister-Bernetta-Quinn.html?soid=1102336588940&aid=Y_WpNPn-XPk.

11 James Wright, *A Wild Perfection: The Selected Letters of James Wright*, ed. Anne Wright and Saundra Rose Maley (Middletown, CT: Wesleyan University Press, 2005), 287.

12 Wright, *Letters*, 287.

13 Wright, 366.

14 Wright, 406.

15 Wright, 406.

16 *The Cloud of Unknowing and Other Works*, trans. A. C. Spearing (New York: Penguin Books, 2001).

17 Stevens, *Letters,* 612.

18 Stevens, 735.

19 Stevens, 735.

20 Stevens, 774.

21 Stevens, 828.

22 Stevens, 752.

23 Stevens, 753.

24 William Carlos Williams, *The Selected Letters of William Carlos Williams*, ed. John C. Thirlwall (New York: New Directions, 1957), 309.

25 Williams, *Letters*, 309.

26 Williams, 337.

27 Sister M. Bernetta Quinn, OSF, "Symbolic Landscape in Frost's 'Nothing Gold Can Stay,'" *The English Journal* 55, no. 5 (May 1966): 624.

28 Sister Bernetta Quinn, OSF, "Twenty-three Ways of Looking at the New Testament—Variations on a Theme," *The Antigonish Review*, accessed July 20, 2022, https://antigonishreview.com/index.php?option=com_content&view=article&id=217:sr-bernetta-quinn-o-s-f&catid=2&Itemid=285.

29 Sister Mary Bernetta Quinn, OSF, "Ernest Pontifex as Anti-hero," *English Literature in Transition, 1880–1920* 5, no. 1 (1962): 31.

30 Flannery O'Connor, *The Habit of Being*, ed. Sally Fitzgerald (New York: Farrar, Straus & Giroux, 1979), 133.

31 Sister M. Bernetta Quinn, OSF, *Dancing in Stillness* (Laurinburg, NC: St. Andrew's Press, 1983), 30.

32 Wright, *Letters*, 177–78.

33 Quinn, *Dancing*, 12.

34 Quinn, 4.

35 Quinn, 8.

36 Quinn, 22.

37 Quinn, 22.

38 Quinn, 22.

39 Quinn, *Metamorphic*, 2.

40 Quinn, 143.

41 Quinn, 3.

42 Sister Bernetta Quinn, "'Paterson': Landscape and Dream," *Journal of Modern Literature* 1, no. 4 (May 1971): 524.

43 Quinn, "Paterson," 524.

44 Quinn, 537.

45 Quinn, *Metamorphic*, 50.

46 Quinn, 61.

47 Quinn, 66.

48 Quinn, 13.

49 Quinn, 9.

50 Quinn, *Dancing*, 25.

51 Quinn, *Metamorphic*, 5.

52 Quinn, *Dancing*, 32.

53 Stevens, *Letters*, 807.

54 Quinn, *Dancing*, 46.

55 Sister M. Bernetta Quinn, OSF, *Ezra Pound: An Introduction to the Poetry* (New York: Columbia University Press, 1972), xii.

56 Quinn, *Pound*, 37.

57 Quinn, 40.

58 Quinn, 43.

59 Sister M. Bernetta Quinn, OSF, "The Terrible Tower Unlocked," *Four Quarters* 8, no. 4 (May 1959): 40.

Chapter 3

1 Louise Bogan, *What the Woman Lived: Selected Letters of Louise Bogan, 1920–1970*, ed. Ruth Limmer (New York: Harcourt Brace Jovanovich, 1973), 338.

2 Bogan, *Woman*, 338.

3 Rosemary Sullivan, "Interview with Madeline DeFrees," in her *Woman Poet* (Reno: Regional Editions, 1980), 45.

4 Bogan, *Woman*, 339.

5 Francis Sweeney, "Poets Speak of Religion," *New York Times*, October 18, 1964, BR51.

6 Sister Mary DeFrees, "The Model Chapel," *The Virginia Quarterly Review* 37, no. 4 (Autumn 1961): 575–90, 575.

7 DeFrees, "Model," 576.

8 DeFrees, 577.

9 "Sister Mary, Poet and Teacher, Is Making Her Mark in Literature," *Washington Post, Times Herald*, October 16, 1965, D10.

10 Jennifer Maier, "A Conversation with Madeline DeFrees," *Image* 61, accessed July 20, 2022, https://imagejournal.org/article/conversation-madeline-defrees/.

11 Madeline DeFrees, *The Springs of Silence* (New York: Prentice-Hall, 1953), 3–4.

12 DeFrees, *Springs*, 5.

13 Maier, "Conversation."

14 Maier, "Conversation."

15 DeFrees, *Springs*, 6.

16 DeFrees, 2.

17 DeFrees, 1.

18 DeFrees, 11.

19 DeFrees, 35.

20 DeFrees, 37.

21 DeFrees, 15.

22 DeFrees, 21.

23 DeFrees, 42.

24 DeFrees, 163.

25 Maier, "Conversation."

26 Maier, "Conversation."

27 Maier, "Conversation."

28 Madeline DeFrees, "Resolution and Independence: John Berryman's Ghost and the Meaning of Life," *The Gettysburg Review*, accessed July 20, 2022, https://www.gettysburgreview.com/selections/detail.dot?inode=070af936-ac3e-447b-8899-a72974295dd7.

29 Maier, "Conversation."

30 DeFrees, "Resolution."

31 DeFrees, *Springs*, 118.

32 DeFrees, 119.

33 DeFrees, 120.

34 Madeline DeFrees, "Early Winter," *New York Times*, January 15, 1958, 28.

35 Madeline DeFrees, "Signals," *New York Times*, November 2, 1959, 30.

36 Tyrone Beason, "Poetic Epiphany," *Seattle Times*, April 4, 2003, E1.

37 Madeline DeFrees (writing as Sister Mary Gilbert), *From the Darkroom* (Indianapolis: The Bobbs-Merrill Company, 1964), 33.

38 DeFrees, *Darkroom*, 32.

39 DeFrees, 40.

40 DeFrees, 40.

41 DeFrees, 48.

42 DeFrees, 35.

43 DeFrees, 35.

44 "Sister Mary, Poet and Teacher."

45 DeFrees, *Darkroom*, 20.

46 DeFrees, 51.

47 DeFrees, *Darkroom*, 11.

48 DeFrees, 13.

49 DeFrees, 46.

50 DeFrees, *Springs*, 104.

51 DeFrees, 106.

52 DeFrees, 111.

53 DeFrees, 113.

54 DeFrees, 148–49.

55 DeFrees, "Resolution."

56 DeFrees, "Resolution."

57   John Berryman, "Eleven Addresses to the Lord," accessed July 20, 2022, https://www.poetryfoundation.org/poems/48948/eleven -addresses-to-the-lord.

58   Berryman, "Eleven."

59   William F. Lynch, SJ, *Christ and Apollo: The Dimensions of the Literary Imagination* (New York: Sheed & Ward, 1960), 50.

60   Philip Coleman and Calista McRae, eds, *The Selected Letters of John Berryman* (Cambridge, MA: The Belknap Press of Harvard University Press, 2022), 313.

61   Coleman and McRae, *Selected Letters,* 314–15.

62   Coleman and McRae, 378.

63   DeFrees, "Resolution."

64   DeFrees, "Resolution."

65   DeFrees, "Resolution."

66   Coleman and McRae, *Selected Letters,* 569.

67   Coleman and McRae, 570.

68   Berryman, "Eleven."

69   Coleman and McRae, *Selected Letters,* 152.

70   Coleman and McRae, 401.

71   Sullivan, "Interview," 45.

72   "Beyond the Convent," *Around the Ring* 3, no. 52 (November 1, 1974): 3.

73   Carol Ann Russell, "An Interview with Madeline DeFrees," *The Massachusetts Review* 23, no. 2 (Summer 1982): 265–69.

74   Madeline DeFrees, "The Radical Activity of Writing Poems," *Northwest Review* 24, no. 2 (January 1986): 52.

75   DeFrees, "Radical," 53.

76   DeFrees, 54.

77   DeFrees, 58.

78   DeFrees, 59–60.

79   DeFrees, 60.

80   Madeline DeFrees, *When Sky Lets Go* (New York: George Braziller, 1978), 31.

81   DeFrees, *Sky,* 38.

82   DeFrees, 62.

83   DeFrees, 41–42.

84   "'Return of the Blue Nun' in Pushcart Prize XLV: 2021," October 16, 2020, accessed July 20, 2022, https://www.madelinedefrees.com /return-of-the-blue-nun-featured-in-pushcart-prize-xlv-2021/.

85 DeFrees, *Sky,* 54.

86 DeFrees, 63.

87 DeFrees, 67.

88 Madeline DeFrees, *The Light Station on Tillamook Rock* (Corvallis, OR: Arrowood Books, 1990), 9.

89 Madeline DeFrees, *Blue Dusk: New & Selected Poems, 1951–2001* (Port Townsend, WA: Copper Canyon Press, 2001), 5.

90 John L'Heureux, *Picnic in Babylon: A Jesuit Priest's Journal, 1963–1967* (New York: The Macmillan Company, 1967), ix.

Chapter 4

1 Arthur F. Kinney, *Flannery O'Connor's Library: Resources of Being* (Athens: The University of Georgia Press, 1985), 117.

2 Flannery O'Connor, *The Habit of Being,* ed. Sally Fitzgerald (New York: Farrar, Straus & Giroux, 1979), 544.

3 Michael Clark, "Sister Criticizes Poetry by Nuns," *New York Times,* October 11, 1959, 115.

4 Clark, "Sister," 115.

5 Clark, 115.

6 Clark, 115.

7 Jennifer Maier, "A Conversation with Madeline DeFrees," *Image* 61, accessed July 20, 2022, https://imagejournal.org/article /conversation-madeline-defrees/.

8 Retta Blaney, "Remembering Sister Maura," *Life Upon the Sacred Stage* (blog), accessed July 21, 2022, http://uponthesacredstage .blogspot.com/2009/11/remembering-sr-maura.html?m=1.

9 Jacques Kelly, "Sister Maura," *Baltimore Sun* obituary, November 18, 2009.

10 Kelly, "Sister Maura."

11 Blaney, "Remembering."

12 Blaney, "Remembering."

13 Sister M. Maura Eichner, SSND, "The Triangle," in *Why I Entered the Convent,* ed. Rev. George L. Kane (Westminster, MD: The Newman Press, 1953), 43.

14 Eichner, "Triangle," 44.

15 Eichner, 45–46.

16 Eichner, 46.

17 Eichner, 46.

18 Eichner, 47.

19 Eichner, 47.

20 Eichner, 49.

21 Sister Maura Eichner, "A Nun Changes Her Habit," *Catholic Digest*, December 1963, accessed July 21, 2022, https://www.sturdyroots.org/file/general-chapters/nun-changes-her-habit-by-maura-eichner-1963.pdf.

22 Blaney, "Remembering."

23 Sister Maura Eichner, "On Reading Dante: The Swinging Bridge," *Improving College and University Teaching* 13, no. 3 (Summer 1965): 189.

24 Peter G. Beidler, ed., *Distinguished Teachers on Effective Teaching* (San Francisco: Jossey-Bass, 1986), 81.

25 Beidler, *Distinguished*, 48.

26 Beidler, 68.

27 Sister Maura Eichner, "Plays Are for Pleasure," *Today* 14, no. 1 (October 1958): 15.

28 Sister Mary Brideen McDonnell, RSM, "Medieval Drama in Catholic Colleges," *America* 89, no. 12 (June 20, 1953): 321.

29 McDonnell, "Medieval," 321.

30 Donald Bremner, "The Maryland College Case: A Clear Test for School Aid," *The Reporter* 32, no. 4 (February 25, 1965): 37.

31 Sister Maura Eichner, "Explication," *The English Journal* 57, no. 1 (January 1968): 20.

32 Sister Maura Eichner, SSND, *After Silence: Selected Poems of Sister Maura Eichner* (Baltimore: Notre Dame of Maryland University, 2011), 150.

33 Edward P. J. Corbett, "The Collegiate Muse: Gone Feminine," *America* 96, no. 9 (December 1, 1956): 265.

34 Corbett, "Collegiate Muse," 265.

35 Corbett, 266.

36 Corbett, 266.

37 Eichner, *After Silence*, 2.

38 Diane Scharper, "Poetic Resurgence Raises Doubts," *Baltimore Sun*, July 23, 1995, accessed August 27, 2022, https://www.baltimoresun.com/news/bs-xpm-1995-07-23-1995204091-story.html.

39 Mary Timothy Prokes, FSE, "'The Feminine Vocation' in Pope John Paul II's Mulieris Dignitatem," *Ave Maria Law Review* 8, no. 1 (Fall 2009): 77–99.

40 Jacques Maritain, "The Apostolate of the Pen," *America* 87, no. 8 (May 24, 1952): 228.

41 Maritain, "Apostolate," 228.

42 Maritain, 228.

43 Maritain, 229.

44 Sister Maura Eichner, "Lesson from the Ancrene Riwle," *America* 87, no. 8 (May 24, 1952): 229.

45 Anne Savage and Nicholas Watson, trans., *Anchoritic Spirituality: Ancrene Wisse and Associated Works* (New York: Paulist Press, 1991), 192.

46 Eichner, "Lesson," 229.

47 Eichner, 229.

48 Eichner, 229.

49 Eichner, 229.

50 Clarence R. Decker and Charles Angoff, "Editorial Notes," *The Literary Review* 1, no. 1 (Fall 1957): *no page number.*

51 Thomas Kretz, "Flesh and Spirit—A Prefatory Note," *The Literary Review* 9, no. 4 (Summer 1966): 546.

52 Sister Maura Eichner, "Look at the World," *Today* 17, no. 5 (February 1962): 17.

53 Eichner, "Look," 19.

54 Sister Maura Eichner, "Make It and Give It Away," *Today* 17, no. 6 (March 1962): 28.

55 Eichner, "Make," 28.

56 Eichner, 27.

57 Eichner, 28.

58 Half-page ad from The Macmillan Company, *America*, May 25, 1946, 159.

59 Eichner, "Triangle," 49.

60 Eichner, *After Silence,* 7.

61 Sister Maura Eichner, "Creativity," *The Literary Review* 9, no. 4 (Summer 1966): 552.

62 Sister Maura Eichner, SSND, "Minimal Score," *Counter/Measures* 3 (1974): 111.

63 Eichner, *After Silence,* 8.

64 Eichner, 9.

65 Eichner, *11.*

66 Eichner, 148.

67 Eichner, 17.

68 Eichner, 17.

69 Eichner, 63.

70 Eichner, 86.

71 Eichner, 161.

72 Sister Maura Eichner, "Parking Lot," *The Literary Review* 9, no. 4 (Summer 1966): 550.

73 Sister Maura Eichner, "Rereading Alan Paton," *The Literary Review* 9, no. 4 (Summer 1966): 551.

74 Sister Maura Eichner, "Advertising," *The Literary Review* 9, no. 4 (Summer 1966): 551.

75 Eichner, "Advertising," 552.

76 Sister Maura Eichner, "Mythopoesis," *The Critic* 20, no. 6. (June–July 1962): 11.

77 Eugene McNamara, "The Word Is Love: Review," *The Critic* 17, no. 4 (February–March 1959): 56.

78 Sister Maura Eichner, "Marginal," *Four Quarters* 5, no. 3 (March 1956): 12.

79 Sister Maura Eichner, "Of Prophecy," *Four Quarters* 8, no. 1 (November 1958): 30.

80 Sister Maura Eichner, "Julie," *Four Quarters* 15, no. 4 (May 1966): 15

81 Sister Maura Eichner, "Woman with Aquarium," *Four Quarters* 17, no. 4 (May 1968): 41.

82 Eichner, *After Silence,* 107.

83 Sister Maura Eichner, "*Dream Songs* Concluded," *Four Quarters* 22, no. 1 (Autumn 1972): 9.

84 Darlene Harbour Unrue, ed., *Katherine Anne Porter Remembered* (Tuscaloosa: The University of Alabama Press, 2010), 211.

85 Unrue, *Porter*, 212.

86 Unrue, 212.

87 Unrue, 213.

88 Sister Maura Eichner, "Visit to Katherine Anne Porter: After the Stroke," *America*, November 15, 1980: 302.

89 Caryle Murphy, "A Final Act of Faith and Charity," *Washington Post*, March 19, 1998, A1.

90 Jacques Kelly, "Sister Maura," *Baltimore Sun*, November 18, 2009, accessed February 22, 2022, https://www.baltimoresun.com/news/bs-xpm-2009-11-18-0911170075-story.html.

91 Murphy, "Final," A1.

92 Eichner, *After Silence,* 163.
93 Eichner, *After Silence,* 2.

Conclusion

1 "Sister Act," *Time,* July 30, 1956, 36.
2 "Sister Act," 36.
3 Sister Mary Francis, *A Right to Be Merry* (New York: Sheed & Ward, 1956), 32.
4 Francis, *A Right,* 127.
5 Mother Mary Angela, PCC, "Biography of Mother Mary Francis, PCC," accessed July 21, 2022, https://poorclares-roswell.org /biography.
6 Kevin Sullivan, "Give Joan a Sword," *Spirit* 11, no. 1 (March 1944): 25.
7 Francis Talbot, SJ, "The Catholic Literary Emergence," *America* 53, no. 13 (July 6, 1935): 305.
8 Talbot, "Catholic," 305.
9 Calvert Alexander, SJ, "Fall Operations on the Literary Front," *America,* 54, no. 1 (1935), 18.
10 Arnold Sparr, *To Promote, Defend, and Redeem: The Catholic Literary Revival and the Cultural Transformation of American Catholicism, 1920–1960* (New York: Greenwood Press, 1990), 17.
11 Sparr, *Promote,* 17.
12 Sparr, 25.
13 Sparr, 25.
14 Sparr, 26.
15 Sparr, 30.
16 Father John Tracy Ellis, "American Catholics and the Intellectual Life," *Thought* 30 (Autumn 1955): 353.
17 Ellis, "American Catholics," 354.
18 Ellis, 355.
19 Ellis, 385.
20 Thomas P. McDonnell, "Criticism and Belief: The Life of the Catholic Critic," *Renascence* 11, no. 2 (Winter 1959): 59.
21 McDonnell, "Criticism," 59.
22 McDonnell, 59.
23 McDonnell, 60.

24 McDonnell, 62.

25 McDonnell, 63.

26 McDonnell, 64.

27 Henry Rago, "Catholics and Literature," *Essays in the American Catholic Tradition*, ed. P. Albert Duhamel (New York: Rinehart & Company, 1960), 209.

28 Henry Rago, "Foreword," *Poetry* 101, no. 1/2 (October–November 1962): ii.

29 Thomas P. Coffey, "Is There an American Catholic Literature?" *Saturday Review*, September 5, 1959, 13.

30 Coffey, "American Catholic," 11.

31 Coffey, 42.

32 Thomas P. McDonnell, "The Nun as Poet," *Spirit* 26, no. 1 (March 1959): 20.

33 McDonnell, "Nun," 20.

34 McDonnell, 20–21.

35 McDonnell, 24.

36 Thomas Merton, "Poetry and Contemplation," in *Essays in the American Catholic Tradition*, ed. P. Albert Duhamel (New York: Rinehart & Company, 1960), 218.

37 Merton, "Poetry," 219.

38 Merton, 227.

39 Gail Porter Mandell, *Madeleva* (Albany: State University of New York Press, 1997), 203.

40 Francis, *Merry*, 129.

41 Francis, 129.

42 Francis, 129.

43 Mother Mary Francis, PCC, *Summon Spirit's Cry* (San Francisco: Ignatius Press, 1996), 25.

44 Francis, *Summon*, 65.

45 Francis, 76.

46 Francis, 100.

47 Francis, 102.

48 McDonnell, "Nun," 21.

49 McDonnell, 22.

50 Francis, *Merry*, 7.

51 Francis, 35.

52 Francis, 37.

53 Francis, 38.

54 Francis, 38.

55 Pope Paul VI, *Perfectae Caritatis*, October 28, 1965, accessed July 21, 2022, https://www.vatican.va/archive/hist_councils/ii _vatican_council/documents/vat-ii_decree_19651028 _perfectae-caritatis_en.html.

56 Mother Mary Francis, PCC, *A Right to Be Merry* (San Francisco: Ignatius Press, 2001) (1973 preface).

57 Francis, *Merry*, 14 (1973 preface).

58 Francis, 13 (1973 preface).

59 Francis, 14 (1973 preface).

60 Francis, *Summon*, 133.

61 Gerard Manley Hopkins, *Poems and Prose*, ed. W. H. Gardner (Baltimore: Penguin Books, 1968), 5.

62 Hopkins, *Poems*, 5.

BIBLIOGRAPHY

Note: Sister Mary Gilbert sometimes published as her birth name, Madeline DeFrees; when she left the convent, she published exclusively as the latter name.

Abbott, Claude Colleer, ed. *The Letters of Gerard Manley Hopkins to Robert Bridges.* London: Oxford University Press, 1935.

Alexander, SJ, Calvert. "Fall Operations on the Literary Front," *America* 54, no. 1 (1935): 17–18.

Angela, PCC, Mother Mary. "Biography of Mother Mary Francis," accessed August 29, 2022, https://poorclares-roswell.org/biography.

Beason, Tyrone. "Poetic Epiphany," *Seattle Times*, April 4, 2003, E1.

Bede. *Historia ecclesiastica gentis Anglorum (Ecclesiastical History of the English People).* Translated by A. M. Sellar. London: George Bell and Sons, 1907.

Beidler, Peter G., ed. *Distinguished Teachers on Effective Teaching.* San Francisco: Jossey-Bass, 1986.

Berryman, John. *The Selected Letters of John Berryman.* Edited by Philip Coleman and Calista McRae. Cambridge, MA: Harvard University Press, 2020.

———. "Eleven Addresses to the Lord," accessed August 5, 2022, https://www.poetryfoundation.org/poems/48948/eleven-addresses-to-the-lord.

Blaney, Retta. "Remembering Sister Maura," *Life Upon the Sacred Stage* (blog), accessed July 21, 2022, http://uponthesacredstage.blogspot.com/2009/11/remembering-sr-maura.html?m=1.

Bogan, Louise. *What the Woman Lived: Selected Letters of Louise Bogan, 1920–1970.* Edited by Ruth Limmer. New York: Harcourt Brace Jovanovich, 1973.

Bremner, Donald. "The Maryland College Case: A Clear Test for School Aid," *The Reporter* 32, no. 4 (February 25, 1965): 37.

Clark, Michael. "Sister Criticizes Poetry by Nuns," *New York Times*, October 11, 1959, 115.

Coffey, Thomas P. "Is There an American Catholic Literature?" *Saturday Review*, September 5, 1959, 11–13.

Connolly, Myles. "Tactics," *America* 54, no. 9 (December 7, 1935): 201–3.

Corbett, Edward P. J. "The Collegiate Muse: Gone Feminine," *America* 96, no. 9 (December 1, 1956): 265–66.

Coulson, Richard P. "A Further View," *Four Quarters* 5, no. 1 (November 1955): 16–20.

Decker, Clarence R., and Charles Angoff. "Editorial Notes," *The Literary Review* 1, no. 1 (Fall 1957): no page number.

DeFrees, Madeline. *Blue Dusk: New & Selected Poems, 1951–2001.* Port Townsend, WA: Copper Canyon Press, 2001.

———. "Resolution and Independence: John Berryman's Ghost and the Meaning of Life, *The Gettysburg Review* 9, no. 7 (Winter 1996): 9–29, accessed August 5, 2022, https://www.gettysburgreview.com/selections/detail.dot?inode=070af936-ac3e-447b-8899-a72974295dd7.

———. *The Light Station on Tillamook Rock.* Corvallis, OR: Arrowood Books, 1990.

———. "The Radical Activity of Writing Poems," *Northwest Review* 24, no. 2 (January 1986): 52–63.

———. *When Sky Lets Go.* New York: George Braziller, 1978.

———. "Mexican Crucifix," *The Sewanee Review* 74, no. 2 (Spring 1966): 419.

———. "Signals," *New York Times*, November 2, 1959, 30.

———. "Early Winter," *New York Times*, January 15, 1958, 28.

———. *The Springs of Silence.* New York: Prentice-Hall, 1953.

DeFrees, SNJM, Sister Mary. "The Model Chapel," *The Virginia Quarterly Review* 37, no. 4 (Autumn 1961): 575–90.

de la Cruz, Sor Juana Inés. *Selected Writings.* Translated by Pamela Kirk Rappaport. New York: Paulist Press, 2005.

———. *Poems, Protest, and a Dream: Selected Writings.* Translated by Margaret Sayers Peden. New York: Penguin Books, 1997.

———. *A Sor Juana Anthology.* Translated by Alan S. Trueblood. Cambridge, MA: Harvard University Press, 1988.

Donohue, John W. "Three Sisters," *America* 180, no. 3 (January 1, 1999): 20.

Dunbar, Judith. "The Sense of Pilgrimage," *America* 178, no. 19 (May 30, 1998): 22–25.

Eichner, SSND, Sister M. Maura. *After Silence: Selected Poems of Sister Maura Eichner.* Baltimore: Notre Dame of Maryland University, 2011.

———. "Visit to Katherine Anne Porter: After the Stroke," *America*, November 15, 1980: 302.

———. "Minimal Score," *Counter/Measures,* no. 3 (1974): 111.

———. "*Dream Songs* Concluded," *Four Quarters* 22, no. 1 (Autumn 1972): 9

———. "Woman with Aquarium," *Four Quarters* 17, no. 4 (May 1968): 41.

———. "Explication," *The English Journal* 57, no. 1 (January 1968): 20.

———. "Advertising," *The Literary Review* 9, no. 4 (Summer 1966): 551.

———. "Creativity," *The Literary Review* 9, no. 4 (Summer 1966): 552.

———. "Parking Lot," *The Literary Review* 9, no. 4 (Summer 1966): 550.

———. "Rereading Alan Paton," *The Literary Review* 9, no. 4 (Summer 1966): 551.

———. "Julie," *Four Quarters* 15, no. 4 (May 1966): 15.

———. "On Reading Dante: The Swinging Bridge," *Improving College and University Teaching* 13, no. 3 (Summer 1965): 188–89.

———. "A Nun Changes Her Habit," *Catholic Digest,* December 1963.

———. "Mythopoesis," *The Critic* 20, no. 6 (June–July 1962): 11

———. "Make It and Give It Away," *Today* 17, no. 6 (March 1962): 28.

———. "Look at the World," *Today* 17, no. 5 (February 1962): 17.

———. "Of Prophecy," *Four Quarters* 8, no. 1 (November 1958): 30.

———. "Plays Are for Pleasure" *Today* 14, no. 1 (October 1958): 15.

———. "Marginal," *Four Quarters* 5, no. 3 (March 1956): 12.

———. "The Triangle." In *Why I Entered the Convent,* edited by Rev. George L. Kane, 43–49. Westminster, MD: The Newman Press, 1953.

————. "Lesson from the Ancrene Riwle," *America* 87, no. 8 (May 24, 1952): 229.

Elgin, Kathleen. *Nun: A Gallery of Sisters.* New York: Random House, 1964.

Ellis, Father John Tracy. "American Catholics and the Intellectual Life," *Thought* 30 (Autumn 1955): 351–88.

Francis PCC, Sister Mary. *A Right to Be Merry.* San Francisco: Ignatius Press, 2001 (1973 preface).

————. *Summon Spirit's Cry.* San Francisco: Ignatius Press, 1996.

————. *A Right to Be Merry.* New York: Sheed & Ward, 1956.

Gilbert, SNJM, Sister Mary. *From the Darkroom.* Indianapolis: The Bobbs-Merrill Company, 1964.

————. "Nuns in Quarterlies," *Poetry Northwest* 2, nos. 1 and 2 (Winter 1960–61): 17–18.

————. "Tumbleweed," *Poetry Northwest* 2, nos. 1 and 2 (Winter 1960–61): 18–19.

Heher, Jack. "Man Seen at His Best 'Thinking About God,'" *Rochester Catholic Courier Journal*, February 28, 1958, 10.

Hodgson, Gege McKay. "Mary Bernetta Quinn," Sisters of Saint Francis, Catholic Sisters Week, March 8–14, 2022, accessed August 5, 2022, https://myemail.constantcontact.com/The-Impact-of-Sister-Bernetta-Quinn.html?soid=1102336588940&aid=Y_WpNPn-XPk.

Hopkins, Gerard Manley. *Poems and Prose.* Edited by W. H. Gardner. Baltimore: Penguin Books, 1968.

Jarrell, Randall. *The Complete Poems.* New York: Farrar, Straus & Giroux, 1969.

Jenks, Barbara C. "Sister Madeleva and Saint Mary's," *The Family Digest* 15, no. 12 (September 1960): 33–35.

Kappes, CST, Marianne. *Track of the Mystic: The Spirituality of Jessica Powers.* Kansas City, MO: Sheed & Ward, 1994.

Kelly, Jacques. "Sister Maura," *Baltimore Sun*, November 18, 2009.

Kinney, Arthur F. *Flannery O'Connor's Library: Resources of Being.* Athens: The University of Georgia Press, 1985.

Kretz, Thomas. "Flesh and Spirit—A Prefatory Note," *The Literary Review* 9, no. 4 (Summer 1966): 546.

Lecky, Dolores R. *Winter Music: A Life of Jessica Powers: Poet, Nun, Woman of the 20th Century.* Kansas City, MO: Sheed & Ward, 1992.

Lees, Clare A., and Gillian R. Overing. *Double Agents: Women and Clerical Culture in Anglo-Saxon England*. Cardiff: University of Wales Press, 2009.

L'Heureux, John. *Picnic in Babylon: A Jesuit Priest's Journal, 1963–1967*. New York: The Macmillan Company, 1967.

Levertov, Denise. "Work That Enfaiths," *CrossCurrents* 40, no. 2 (Summer 1990): 150–59.

———. "Cædmon," *Southern Humanities Review* 19, no. 3 (Summer 1985): 203.

Lynch, SJ, William F. *Christ and Apollo: The Dimensions of the Literary Imagination*. New York: Sheed & Ward, 1960.

Maier, Jennifer. "A Conversation with Madeline DeFrees," *Image Journal* 61, accessed July 20, 2022, https://imagejournal.org/article/conversation-madeline-defrees/.

Mandell, Gail Porter. *Madeleva*. Albany: State University of New York Press, 1997.

Mariani, Paul. *Gerard Manley Hopkins: A Life*. New York: Viking, 2008.

Maritain, Jacques. "The Apostolate of the Pen," *America* 87, no. 8 (May 24, 1952): 228–29.

McDonnell, RSM, Sister Mary Brideen. "Medieval Drama in Catholic Colleges," *America* 89, no. 12 (June 20, 1953): 320–21.

McDonnell, Thomas P. "Criticism and Belief: The Life of the Catholic Critic," *Renascence* 11, no. 2 (Winter 1959): 59–64.

———. "The Nun as Poet," *Spirit* 26, no. 1 (March 1959): 21–25.

McNamara, Eugene. "The Word Is Love: Review," *The Critic* 17, no. 4 (February–March 1959): 56.

Merton, Thomas. "Poetry and Contemplation." In *Essays in the American Catholic Tradition*, edited by P. Albert Duhamel, 214–28. New York: Rinehart & Company, 1960.

Meyers, Sister Bertrande. *Sisters for the 21st Century*. New York: Sheed & Ward, 1965.

Michelson, Peter. "On the Purple Sage, Chicago Review, and Big Table." In *The Little Magazine in America: A Modern Documentary History*, edited by Elliott Anderson and Mary Kinzie, 341–75. Yonkers, NY: Pushcart, 1978.

Morneau, Robert F. *Mantras from a Poet: Jessica Powers*. Kansas City, MO: Sheed & Ward, 1991.

Murphy, Caryle. "A Final Act of Faith and Charity," *Washington Post*, March 19, 1998, A1.

Oates, Mary J. *Pursuing Truth: How Gender Shaped Catholic Education at the College of Notre Dame of Maryland.* Ithaca, NY: Cornell University Press, 2021.

O'Connor, Flannery. *The Habit of Being.* Edited by Sally Fitzgerald. New York: Farrar, Straus & Giroux, 1979.

Patrick, FSC, Brother Felician. "Symposium," *Four Quarters* 10, no. 2 (January 1961): 17

———. "Survey of Responses and Introduction to the Series," *Four Quarters* 10, no. 1 (November 1960): 9–17.

Paz, Octavio. *Sor Juana, or, the Traps of Faith.* Translated by Margaret Sayers Peden. Cambridge, MA: Harvard University Press, 1988.

Pollak, Felix. "The World of Literary Magazines." In *Paper Dreams: Writers and Editors on the American Literary Magazine*, edited by Travis Kurowski, 159–66. Madison, NJ: Atticus Books, 2013.

Pope Paul VI. *Perfectae Caritatis,* October 28, 1965, accessed August 5, 2022, https://www.vatican.va/archive/hist_councils/ii_vatican _council/documents/vat-ii_decree_19651028_perfectae -caritatis_en.html.

Pound, Ezra. "Small Magazines," *The English Journal* 19, no. 9 (November 1930): 689–704.

Powers, Jessica. *Selected Poetry of Jessica Powers.* Edited by Regina Siegfried, ASC and Robert F. Morneau. Kansas City, MO: Sheed & Ward, 1991.

Prokes, FSE, Mary Timothy. "'The Feminine Vocation' in Pope John Paul II's Mulieris Dignitatem," *Ave Maria Law Review* 8, no. 1 (Fall 2009): 77–99.

Quinn, OSF, Sister M. Bernetta. *Dancing in Stillness.* Laurinburg, NC: St. Andrews Press, 1983.

———. *Randall Jarrell.* Boston: Twayne Publishers, 1981.

———. *Ezra Pound: An Introduction to the Poetry.* New York: Columbia University Press, 1972.

———. "'Paterson': Landscape and Dream," *Journal of Modern Literature* 1, no. 4 (May 1971): 523–48.

———. "Symbolic Landscape in Frost's 'Nothing Gold Can Stay,'" *The English Journal* 55, no. 5 (May 1966): 621–24.

———. *The Metamorphic Tradition in Modern Poetry.* New York: Gordian Press, 1966.

———. "Ernest Pontifex as Anti-hero," *English Literature in Transition, 1880–1920* 5, no. 1 (1962): 31.

———. "The Terrible Tower Unlocked," *Four Quarters* 8, no. 4 (May 1959): 40.

———. *Design in Gold: A History of the College of Saint Teresa.* Winona, MN: College of Saint Teresa, 1957.

———. "Twenty-three Ways of Looking at the New Testament: Variations on a Theme," *The Antigonish Review,* accessed August 5, 2022, https://antigonishreview.com/index.php?option=com _content&view=article&id=217:sr-bernetta-quinn-o-s -f&catid=2&Itemid=285.

Rago, Henry. "Foreword," *Poetry* 101, no. 1/2 (October–November 1962): ii.

———. "Catholics and Literature." In *Essays in the American Catholic Tradition,* edited by P. Albert Duhamel, 208–14. New York: Rinehart & Company, 1960.

Russell, Carol Ann. "An Interview with Madeline DeFrees," *The Massachusetts Review* 23, no. 2 (Summer 1982): 265–69.

Savage, Anne, and Nicholas Watson, trans. *Anchoritic Spirituality: Ancrene Wisse and Associated Works.* New York: Paulist Press, 1991.

Scharper, Diane. "Poetic Resurgence Raises Doubts," *Baltimore Sun,* July 23, 1995, :https://www.baltimoresun.com/news/bs-xpm-1995-07-23-1995204091-story.html

Secrest, Meryle. "Modern Literature Lacks Old Ideals," *Washington Post,* July 7, 1962, A11.

Sparr, Arnold. *To Promote, Defend, and Redeem: The Catholic Literary Revival and the Cultural Transformation of American Catholicism, 1920–1960.* New York: Greenwood Press, 1990.

Spearing, A. C., trans. *The Cloud of Unknowing and Other Works.* New York: Penguin Books, 2001.

Stevens, Wallace. *The Letters of Wallace Stevens.* Edited by Holly Stevens. New York: Knopf Doubleday, 1966.

Sullivan, Kevin. "Give Joan a Sword," *Spirit* 11, no. 1 (March 1944): 25.

Sullivan, Rosemary. "Interview with Madeline DeFrees." In *Woman Poet*, 45–47. Reno: Regional Editions, 1980.

Sweeney, Francis. "Poets Speak of Religion," *New York Times*, October 18, 1964, BR51.

Talbot, SJ, Francis. "The Catholic Literary Emergence," *America* 53, no. 13 (July 6, 1935): 304–5.

Unrue, Darlene Harbour, ed. *Katherine Anne Porter Remembered*. Tuscaloosa: The University of Alabama Press, 2010.

Williams, William Carlos. *The Selected Letters of William Carlos Williams*. Edited by John C. Thirlwall. New York: New Directions, 1957.

Wills, Garry. "Women Who Defied Fate," *New York Times*, December 21, 1980, BR1.

Wolff, CSC, Madeleva. *Chaucer's Nuns, and Other Essays*. Port Washington, NY: Kennikat Press, 1965.

———. *The Four Last Things: Collected Poems*. New York: Macmillan, 1959.

———. *My First Seventy Years*. New York: Macmillan, 1959.

———. "The Education of Our Young Religious Teachers," *Bulletin: National Catholic Educational Association* 46, no. 1 (August 1949): 253–56.

Wright, James. *A Wild Perfection: The Selected Letters of James Wright*. Edited by Anne Wright and Saundra Rose Maley. Middletown, CT: Wesleyan University Press, 2005.

Zaturenska, Marya. "Music That Is Peace," *New York Times*, February 15, 1948, BR6.

Works with no listed authors

"About the Contributors," *Poetry Northwest* 2, no. 3 (Summer 1961).

"Announcement," *Four Quarters* 1, no. 1 (November 1951): 1.

"Beyond the Convent," *Around the Ring* 3, no. 52 (November 1, 1974): 3.

"Catholic Poetry Society Launched," *The Catholic Transcript*, April 2, 1931, 9.

"Journalistic Nun Pursues Studies," *New York Times,* March 29, 1964, 62.

"A Nun Appraises Modern Poets," *Buffalo Evening News*, Wednesday, April 25, 1962, 49.

"Nun-poetess Sees End of Free-verse Period," *Los Angeles Times*, May 7, 1932, A9.

"Nun, President and Poet," *Life*, June 10, 1957, 130.

"Sister Act," *Time*, July 30, 1956, 36.

"Sister Mary, Poet and Teacher, Is Making Her Mark in Literature," *Washington Post*, October 16, 1965, D10.

"Who's Who," *America*, April 9, 1938, 1.

INDEX

Abraham, 26–27, 72
Ahlgren, Gillian T.W., xvi
Alexander, SJ, Calvert, 79
Allen University, 33
America, 19, 20, 22, 46, 65, 67, 70, 79–80
Atlantic Monthly, 65–66

Barth, John, 8
Bede, x
Belloc, Hilaire, 80, 87
Beloit Poetry Journal, 46
Benedictine, 53
Berryman, John, 49, 53–56, 75
Bethlehem, 28
Bible, 16, 65, 74
Bishop, Elizabeth, xiv
Bogan, Louise, 45
Book of Revelation, 35
Boston College, 11
Boston Globe, 82
Bradbury, Ray, 14
Brogan, Denis W., 81
Brunini, John, 19

Caedmon, ix–xi, xvii
California (at Berkeley), University of, 5, 9, 12
Carmel of the Mother of God Monastery, 23
Carmleite, 24–25, 30, 38

Catholic Poetry Society of America, 12, 19, 20, 61
Catholic University of America, 33, 81
Catholic Worker, The, 20
Cenacle Sister, 19
Chaucer, Geoffrey, 9, 11
Chesterton, G.K., 12, 20
Christian Brothers, 4, 58
Ciardi, John, 69
Coffey, Thomas P., 85
College of Notre Dame of Maryland, 61, 64, 66
College of St. Teresa, 32–33, 37
Coltrane, John, 39
Commonweal, 5
Connolly, Myles, 20–22, 69, 80, 81, 85
Corbett, Edward P.J., 65–66
Crane, Hart, 33
Creighton University, 65
Cummings, E.E., 69

Daniel, xiv
Dante, 41, 64
Daughters of Charity, 12
de la Cruz, Sor Juana Inés, xiii–xvii
de la Laguna, Marqués, xv
DeFrees, Madeline (Sister Mary Gilbert), 1, 45–60, 62, 69, 75, 90

DePaul University, 79
Dickinson, Emily, xiii–xiv
Dominican, 23, 24, 54, 88
Donohue, SJ, John W., 11–12
Doyle, John W., 65
Du Bos, Charles, 83

Egoist, The, 2
Elijah, 27
Eliot, T.S., 8, 11, 33, 39
Elizabeth, 70
Ellis, Father John Tracy, 81
Everson, William, 54, 88

Fairleigh Dickinson University,
    68
Faulkner, William, 9
Fordham University, 20, 54, 85
Four Quarters, 4, 14, 73–74
Franciscan, xi, 39
Franciscan Sister of the Congre-
    gation of Our Lady of
    Lourdes, 32, 89
Frost, Robert, 11, 36, 57

Gardner, Isabella, 54
Giroux, Robert, 55
Goethe, Johann Wolfgang von,
    6, 7
Gordimer, Nadine, 8
Graves, Morris, 1
Greenbaum, Joseph J., 81
Guggenheim Fellowship, 59
Gunn, Thom, 1

H.D., 2
Hall, Donald, 1, 69
Hallen, Marilynn, 33

Hazo, Samuel, 45
Heaney, Seamus, 34
Hemingway, Ernest, 2, 9, 57
Hemschemeyer, Hattie, 63
Hilda, x, xvii, 43
Holy Names College, 1, 46
Hopkins, Gerard Manley,
    ix, x–xiii, xvii, 20, 29, 41,
    56, 90
Howard, Jane, 55
Hughes, Langston, 69
Hughes, Ted, 67
Hugo, Richard, 53
Hurd, Peter, 33

Indiana University, 49, 53
International Yeats Summer
    School, 33

Jarrell, Randall, 31, 33, 42
Jebb, Eleanor, 87
Jerusalem, xiv
Jesuit, xi, xii, xvi, xvii, 19, 20,
    24, 37, 47, 54, 55, 60, 66,
    69, 78–79, 82, 84, 89
Jesus, 27, 45, 54, 71, 72
John the Baptist, 70
Jones, SJ, James, xii
Jordan, Elizabeth, 7
Joyce, James, 2, 4, 9, 40

Kennedy, John F., 14, 36
Kenny, Herbert Andrew,
    82–83
Kerith Ravine, 27
Kilmer, Aline, 19
Kilmer, Joyce, 10, 19
Knapp, Robert H., 81

Kretz, Thomas, 69
Kunitz, Stanley, 1, 45

La Salle College, 4, 73
Larkin, Philip, 1
Leo House, 19
Levertov, Denise, ix, x, 34
Levi, Peter, 69
Levine, Ann, 54
Levine, Philip, 1
Lewis, C.S., 5
L'Heureux, John, 60
Life, 6, 10, 12,
Literary Review, The, 68–69, 73
Little Review, 2
Loyola University, Chicago, 69
Lowell, Robert, 8, 45, 54,
Luisa, María, xv
Lynch, SJ, William F., 54

MacDowell Colony, 33
Maritain, Jacques, 67, 69, 80, 81
Marquette University, 24, 82
Mary (Blessed Mother), xiv, 16,
    41, 71
Maryknoll Sisters, xiii
Marylhurst College, 47
Massart, Sister Lucille, 23–24
Maynard, Theodore, 80
McDonnell, Thomas P., 82–83,
    86–87
McKay, Claude, 54
Meiji Gakuin University, 33
Merton, Thomas, 6, 8, 15, 81,
    82, 86–87
Michener, James, 14
Miller, Arthur, 4, 46
Minnesota Review, 46

Mistral, Gabriela, xiv, 69
Moeller, Charles, 83
Monastery of the Poor Clares, 77
Moore, Marianne, xiv, 2
Morrison, Toni, 57

Nash, Ogden, 11
National Catholic Educational
    Association, 12–13
National Endowment for the
    Arts, 33
National Endowment for the
    Humanities, 33
New Age, 2
New Republic, The, 5
New York Times, 5, 20, 46
Newman, Cardinal Henry, x
Norfolk State University, 33
Northwest Review, 46

O'Connor, Flannery, 8, 14, 37,
    46, 61, 62
O'Donnell, Father Charles, 10
O'Hara, John, 14
Our Lady of Mount Carmel, 25
Ovid, 40
Oxford, 5, 9

Patrick, Brother Felician, 14
Paz, Octavio, xiii, xv
Pegis, Anton Charles, 20
Pegis, Jessie, 20
Percy, Walker, 81, 85
Pollak, Felix, 3, 9
Porter, Katherine Anne, 14,
    75–76
Pound, Ezra, 2–3, 9, 33, 43
Powell, Christopher, 24

Powers, Jessica, 14, 19–30, 86, 90
Pynchon, Thomas, 8
Poetry, 2, 82–83
Poetry Northwest, 1, 46
Poor Clares, 77
Pope, Alexander, 63
Powers, J.F., 8, 39, 85
Prairie Schooner, 46
Proust, Marcel, 4

Rago, Henry, 82–84
Rahner, Karl, 81
Renascence, 8, 82
Rexroth, Kenneth, 54
Roethke, Theodore, 37
Rogers, Daniel, 69
Roseliep, Father Raymond, 69

Saint Augustine, 59, 74, 75
Saint Beuno's College, xi
Saint Clare, 90
Saint John of the Cross, 25, 88
Saint Louis University, 12, 89
Saint Mary's College, 5, 7, 12
Saint Paul, 40
Saint Peter's University, 85
Saturday Review, The, 85
School Sisters of Notre Dame, 63, 76
Seattle University, 46
Second Vatican Council, 12, 89
Seidel, Frederick, 45
Sewanee Review, The, 32, 46, 57
Sexton, Anne, 1
Sheed, Frank, 78
Sheed & Ward, 20, 78
Sheen, Monsignor Fulton J., 80

Siena College, 33
Simon of Cyrene, 24
Sister Bertrande Myers, 12–13
Sister Formation Conference, 13
Sister Kathleen Feeley, 75
Sister M. Sebastian, 69
Sister Maria del Rey, xiii
Sister Mary Bernetta Quinn, 31–43, 90
Sister Mary Francis, 77–78, 86, 87–90
Sister Mary Hester, 69
Sister Mary Jeremy, 69
Sister Mary Joseph Scherer, 79–80
Sister Mary Roman, 77
Sister Maura Eichner, 13, 14, 61–76, 78, 86, 90
Sister Rita Heffernan, 7
Sisters of the Holy Cross, 7
Sisters of Holy Names of Jesus and Mary, 1, 45
Sisters of Loretto, 79
Sisters of Saint Agnes, 19
Sisters of Saint Joseph, 53
Sisters of Saint Mary, 47
Sparr, Arnold, 80–81
Spirit, 19, 46, 50, 86
Stafford, Jean, 8
Stafford, William, 1
Stein, Gertrude, 9
Stevens, Wallace, 2, 31–32, 33, 34, 35–37, 40, 42
SUNY-Buffalo, 33
Surles, Eileen, 19

Talbot, SJ, Francis Xavier, 79–81
Tate, Allen, 4, 33, 54

Teresa of Ávila, 30
Thomas, Dylan, 8
Thought, 81
Today, National Catholic Magazine, 69
Tolkien, J.R.R., 5

Undset, Sigrid, 80
University of Chicago, 82, 84
University of Massachusetts, Amherst, 59
University of Montana, 53, 58, 59
University of Oregon, 47, 53
University of Pittsburgh, xiii
University of the Sacred Heart, 33
University of Wisconsin, 6, 31, 32

Updike, John, 46

Veronica, 37, 72, 78
Virginia Quarterly Review, 46

Warren, Robert Penn, 8, 34, 51
Webster College, 79–80
White, Natalie E., 77
Whitman, Walt, 55
Williams, William Carlos, 2, 8, 33, 34, 36, 39, 40, 42, 69
Wills, Garry, 12
Wolff, Sister Madeleva, 1–18, 19, 62, 80, 87, 90
Wood, Allyn, 1
Wright, James, 34–35

Yaddo, 33
Yeats, W.B., 33, 39, 40